P9-BXV-891

FIRST IMPRESSIONS

EFFECTIVE CHURCH SERIES

ROBERT A. LEE
Edited by HERB MILLER

FIRST IMPRESSIONS

ABINGDON PRESS

Nashville

FIRST IMPRESSIONS

Copyright © 1993 by Abingdon Press

All rights reserved.
No part of this work may be reproduced or transmitted in any form or by any means, electronic or mechanical, including photocopying and recording, or by any information storage or retrieval system, except as may be expressly permitted by the 1976 Copyright Act or in writing to Abingdon Press, 201 Eighth Avenue South, P.O. Box 801, Nashville, TN 37202.

This book is printed on acid-free, recycled paper.

Library of Congress Cataloging-in-Publication Data

Lee, Robert A.
  First impressions/Robert A. Lee.
    p. cm.—(Effective church series)
  Includes bibliographical references.
  ISBN 0-687-07855-5 (alk. paper)
  1. Church maintenance and repair. I. Title. II. Series.
BV652.7.L44   1993
254'.7—dc20   93-12891
                                                              CIP

93 94 95 96 97 98 99 00 01 02   —   10 9 8 7 6 5 4 3 2 1

MANUFACTURED IN THE UNITED STATES OF AMERICA

To former clients,
who have made church architecture
much more than a job.
It has been a great joy.

89004

CONTENTS

FOREWORD

Parked by a busy street, the pink van lacked its left rear tire. A jack held the vehicle off the pavement at a crazy angle. "For Sale" said a sign in the back window. The van's owner surely did not plan this strategy. Passersby got a beautiful illustration of poor advertising at its worst.

Churches are not in sales; they are in the giving business. But buildings influence how well congregations give away the most valuable gift human lives can receive. Because the appearance of the building's interior and exterior is either inviting or uninviting, it makes an impact in major ways: (1) how many people show up to investigate the potential value of the gift; (2) what percentage of the guests decide to return for future consideration of the gift; (3) the number of visitors who experience a life-changing connection with Jesus Christ; and (4) the depth to which those who connect grow spiritually in that relationship.

Few church buildings present the extreme negative image of a pink van with a flat tire. But leaders can strengthen every building's internal and external visual impact—often at minor cost. Most books by architects talk solely about creating new buildings. A few other such books focus on remodeling. In *First Impressions*, Robert Lee's unique insights extend far beyond those standard patterns. His checklist provides a church building physical. By reading and discussing the chapters, one per month, committee members can analyze their buildings and make plans for raising them to maximum inviting and spiritual nurture effectiveness.

Lee's leadership insights fit the goal of the Effective Church Series: to help meet the need for "how-to" answers in specific areas of church life. Each of these volumes provides clergy and laypersons with practical insights and methods that can increase their congregation's effectiveness in achieving God's purposes in every aspect of ministry: leadership, worship, Sunday school, membership care, biblical literacy, spiritual growth, small groups, evangelism, new-member assimilation, prayer, youth work, singles work, young adult work, time management, stewardship, administration, community service, world mission, conflict resolution, and writing skills.

Lee's insights also fit the theological focus of the Effective Church Series. While concentrating more on the practical "how to do it" than on the theoretical and conceptual, these "ideas that work" rest on biblical principles. Without that foundation, method sharing feeds us a diet of cotton candy, sweet but without nutrients. Lee has addressed the subject of inviting buildings in ways consistent with biblical truths and classic Christian theology.

A convention speaker in Canada was proud of his new monogrammed shirt. The left cuff carried his initials in a rich navy color that contrasted beautifully with the white broadcloth. After his address, he sat down on the front row of the auditorium as the master of ceremonies took the podium to make lunch announcements. A woman on the row behind the speaker reached up and tapped his arm. "What is that?" she said.

"What?" he replied.

"On your shirt sleeve?" she asked.

He showed her, "Oh," she said, "I thought it was L for left."

Some endeavors do not require detailed instructions.

Others are far more technical. Church buildings fall into the latter category. Leaders need expert insights on how their church can continue to accomplish the mission for which it was built. Lee gives that insight in interesting, practical ways.

Herb Miller
Lubbock, Texas

I

WHY EVALUATE YOUR FACILITIES?

"Leave It to Beaver" was one of the favorite television shows of the 1950s. Families liked to watch how the almost-perfect Cleaver family—a father, a mother, and two sons—dealt with their joys and sorrows. June Cleaver did not work outside the home, and her children's challenges did not include guns and drugs. Today people tune in to television shows about working women, single-parent families, blended families, and every other family configuration. Violence, pollution, abuse, dysfunctional families, AIDS, and homelessness set a much more complex and challenging cultural scene than did June Cleaver's kitchen.

These contrasts demonstrate the differences between two generations. While the video medium has adjusted to the sociological changes in the last thirty years, many of our churches have not. Although churches struggle to meet the needs of all generations, the older generation is generally well fed, while the younger group is largely undernourished.

Seventy-seven Million "Very Different" People

God is trying to connect with seventy-seven million people in America born between 1946 and 1964. Now called the baby boom generation, they are different. But how are they different? Why do only 40 percent of them regularly attend a religious service?

Baby boomers are noted for consumerism, sensuality, progressiveness, and loneliness. These characteristics have a profound influence on churches. Dozens of publications address the changes needed in various types of ministries. This book guides church leaders in strengthening the effectiveness of the *facilities* in which these ministries occur. It provides a road map for the nearly 375,000 church property committees that need a diagnostic process to help their churches become more "ministry friendly" when reaching out to the younger generations.

Now Is the Time

According to sociologists, baby boomers are returning to churches in droves. They are reevaluating their lives and are more interested in religion than ever before. With young families in hand, many are returning, but they are asking, "What is in it for me?" They will attend a church of just about any denomination, as long as it fulfills their needs. If a congregation does not satisfy them, they go down the street to a different church or to the golf course, or they just sleep in on Sunday morning.

We can rail against shallow theology and supermarket religion, but we cannot help people grow in their faith and become committed disciples of Christ unless we can reach them first. *Now is the time* for churches to seek out these people. By the age of forty-five, most baby boomers have established their churchgoing habits. If church leaders miss this opportunity, they will lose up to fifty million people, plus their millions of children in the next generation.

A Facility Physical

As we get older, our bodies tend to wear out and malfunction. That is why the medical community urges us to have more regular checkups as we age. We all want to be as

14

healthy and useful as possible. Our church facilities age as well. From wear and tear, they tend to become less useful. But something else also diminishes their effectiveness—a changing society.

Let us, therefore, give your building a quick physical to evaluate its present usefulness. Does your church facility have any of the following symptoms? Are the symptoms an indication of a major illness or just a minor ailment? (Be sure to ask the following questions of members in their thirties and forties, as well as the established older members of your congregation. Also, try to obtain a response to these questions from non-churchgoing members of your community.)

1. Does the building look contemporary and attractive to baby boomers?
2. Have we updated a significant building element in the last two years?
3. In the last year, have we planned our next remodeling project?

If you answered no to any of these questions, examine your building more thoroughly. Take a careful look at the symptoms. Does it have a minor illness that can be cured with a new exterior sign? Or does it have a disorder requiring major surgery, like the renovation of, or an addition to, your lobby? Either scenario requires some careful evaluation and action. A sickly building can cause a decreasing ministry to boomers and their families.

The Prodigal Generation

As the prodigal son returned home in Jesus' parable, the father ordered a great celebration. He gave the boy a position of great prominence. He received royal treatment with jubilant music, dancing, feasting, and rich clothes and jewelry. From God's perspective, do not baby boomers who return to church after abandoning it in their teens also deserve a celebration? Maybe more of them would return if churches treated them as prodigal children of God.

15

How can churches respond to the needs of these young people? A good doctor always tries to understand the total circumstances of a patient's life before diagnosing an illness. So let us step back and get some perspective on how baby boomers define themselves.

1. They are very consumer oriented. Trained to shop carefully and invest wisely, they have learned to compare values. To impress boomers, you need to satisfy their needs. They are also impatient, so you must satisfy their needs quickly. They demand *convenience.* You cannot pamper these consumers enough. How close is the parking space to the entrance? How difficult is the journey to the nursery? Boomers who are new to a church want to be served, not to be serving. They also demand *compliance.* Boomers have many expectations and demands. You will either satisfy their preconceptions or be relegated to a no-win situation. Boomers expect church buildings to work like the rest of our society—that is, the hospitality of a hotel, the fun of a recreation center, the sumptuous food of a restaurant, the professionalism of a good preschool. If a building is very user friendly and functional, then people will consider "buying" your ministry. If not, many of them will "shop" elsewhere. They expect to be satisfied when they go to church. And, as a shampoo ad reminds us, "You never get a second chance at a first impression."

2. Boomers are very sensual. They go for the experience. How are their senses involved and tantalized? Is going to church fun? To understand this principle, watch television, listen to the radio, and see the magazines that boomers read. The music is involving, the magazines are colorful, and the videos are hypnotic. All of their media must mesmerize and captivate.

That is your competition. Does your building press the baby boomers' hot buttons? They demand *cheerfulness.* Bright colors and people-pleasing elements such as textured walks, indoor and outdoor landscaping, artwork, and soothing lighting are some examples. They also demand *comfort.* Hard, cold, dull, harsh, institutional, overheated, and unapproachable are all elements to be avoided. A building must be like the wrapping paper on a Christmas present in order to satisfy their sensual desires. The packaging sells the product and sets the stage for the experience. Without proper packaging, the gift never gets opened.

3. Baby boomers are progressive. Why is it that boomers do not use slide rules anymore? You remember slide rules—they are the number-covered instruments used to calculate complex math formulas. Now we purchase computers or calculators to solve our numerical problems. Experts say that we have had more changes in technology in the last fifty years than the generations before us saw in the previous five hundred years. McDonald's has modernized and added variety to its store designs because boomers get bored with sameness. Television reruns are very dull to most people. Does your building have the look of a rerun? How old does your building look? How old does it feel? How old does it work? Boomers want *contemporary,* and they want *variety.*

In Jesus' time, only a fool would put new wine in an old leather container (Matt. 9:17). The new wine would burst the old skin. Therefore, both the wine and the wineskin would be wasted. Wise people combined new wine and new wineskins to preserve the effectiveness of both. A wise property committee will not try to force new younger adult members into an outdated, old-feeling facility.

4. Boomers are lonely. Besides computers and calculators, boomers use mobile phones, copy machines, modems, and FAX machines to increase the efficiency in their lives. While these machines improve productivity, they also increase isolation. Couple the high-tech machinery with a highly mobile society and a society where people often use others in order to get to the top, and you understand why baby boomers are plagued by loneliness. How can church buildings increase the sense of belonging for lonely people? By encouraging human *contact* and *connection* between people. An airline commercial demonstrates this principle. It describes a company losing its market share because it depends too much on technology to sell its product. Its customers felt unwanted and isolated from the sales staff. To improve relations and strengthen connections and maintain sales, the company decided to send all of its sales personnel to meet the clients face-to-face. The same is true of church buildings that bring people together. They help destroy the walls around people. They also build bridges to the neighbors we are to love (Mark 12:31). Helping people see, feel, and hear each other is the greatest achievement a building can provide.

"Love one another with mutual affection; outdo one another in showing honor. . . . Contribute to the needs of the saints; extend hospitality to strangers. . . . Rejoice with those who rejoice, weep with those who weep . . . associate with the lowly. . . . If it is possible, so far as it depends on you, live peaceably with all" (Rom. 12:9-21). Can you sense the human contact? "All who believed were together and had all things in common; they would sell their possessions and goods and distribute the proceeds to all, as any had need" (Acts 2:44-45). Can you sense the human caring? Church buildings that reinforce these attitudes focus people on people.

God's Real House

Our society is experiencing major sociological shifts. As a "facilities doctor," every pastor, church leader, and property committee must consider the negative consequences that outdated and ill-equipped facilities have on a ministry. A sickly facility will probably produce an unhealthy ministry. Conversely, a healthy facility will improve a church's ministry capabilities.

Your facilities are tools to build God's real house—the people. This a great responsibility, but it also gives you a great opportunity to build up this generation into a "spiritual house"—a house that will "offer spiritual sacrifices acceptable to God through Jesus Christ" (1 Peter 2:4-5).

It is true that church architecture will have little consequence in heaven. Buildings are temporary structures for people to meet God and his people in. On the other hand, they are important elements in a healthy church's ministry. With this book, I hope to strengthen your kingdom-making ministry by showing you how your church structure can work for you.

✜

II

THE TOP TWENTY IMPROVEMENTS FOR UNDER THREE HUNDRED DOLLARS

Some of the best building improvements are like Jesus' parable of the treasure hidden in a field. After finding the treasure, the man sells all he owns to buy the field. He gets much more in the treasure than he paid for the field and, therefore, makes a profit (Matt. 13:44).

The top twenty building improvements for under three hundred dollars allow a church to have its cake and eat it too. Since they cost less than three hundred dollars, these improvements will not hamper the funding of ministries. Yet, they will add to a church's ministry the way a cake adds to the excitement and enjoyment of a birthday party. These effective, yet inexpensive, ideas add the quality needed to minister to all church members, including baby boomers.

An Exalting Exterior

Boomers are consumers. They want cheerfulness and change. Therefore, they want colorful church facilities. They desire vibrant, bright, positive, flashy "wrappings" on the places they visit. As you drive around your city, notice how shopping centers express these attitudes. How have they incorporated the "wrapping paper" into the design of their buildings and landscaped areas?

In the summer they do it with colorful landscaping. Trees, flowers, and other plants animate the world we want to enjoy. Go to any theme park and you will see vivid examples. They are vibrant in color, with intoxicating aromas and rhythmic movements in the wind. Obviously, most churches do not have the budget or time to duplicate the intensity of landscaping in these theme parks. But most churches can build a colorful reputation for under three hundred dollars. A church in south Denver has been known as the "pink petunia church" over the last few years. In the spring time they plant a few hundred petunias around their sign and at the entrances to their parking lot. This massive planting is more effective than any church sign because it builds a glorious reputation.

The winter requires a different scenario. During long, dark nights and cold blustery weather, retail centers use twinkling lights to illuminate and warm people's attitudes. Yet, most churches are as dark and drab as the weather. Even though this is the most celebrated season (with Thanksgiving and Christmas), few churches demonstrate "joy to the world." A couple of hundred dollars worth of decorative lights go a long way toward attracting the baby boomers. Try outlining your building or wrapping the landscaping. Decorating with a lighted star or an angel is an outstanding idea, but the lights do not have to represent anything. The main intent is to come across as positive, warmhearted, and inviting.

A word of caution: Some churches get a great idea and use it so long that it becomes dull and lifeless. Remember that baby boomers like change. So keep the wrapping paper fresh. Alter the ideas without altering the intent. Change the colors on the landscaping and lights. Add a manger scene. Go from pink petunias to blue daisies. Add a new tree or a cross and empty tomb scene at Easter. Try to change at least one element of your design every season.

Precious Parking

Most churches built before the automobile became the dominant mode of transportation have a parking shortage.

The boomer generation averages 2.2 cars per family, and they seem to bring all of them to church. Also, the family units are getting smaller (because of lower birth rates and single-parent families), so a 500-person facility now requires at least 250 parking spaces instead of the 100 needed only fifteen years ago. Therefore, the parking ratio should be at least one space for every two sanctuary seats. If you have overlapping services, or one audience lingers around after a second has arrived, then the parking should be increased accordingly. Lastly, visitors demand convenience in parking. If they cannot find a space quickly, or if it is one block away, many of them will become disgruntled and leave before they can experience a church's great service.

To help satisfy people's infatuation with their automobiles, you may improve your church's parking by: (1) reserving spaces for visitor parking near the front door, and post signs. The proper amount of visitor parking is at least 4 percent of your total parking and not fewer than three visitor spaces. (?) If your lot is too small, park the cars of members in stacking parking stalls. By eliminating some of the aisles, you could add 50 to 60 percent to your parking. And this can be done without spending a dime. Although this is a complex logistical scheme, it can add to the friendliness of your church. Give parking stickers to members, then lot attendants can direct them to the stacked spots. Direct the unmarked cars of nonmembers to the privileged spots where greeters welcome them. Several churches in California use this scheme successfully. It not only adds parking, but it also welcomes visitors, and it is accomplished with little funding. It also provides the convenience, human contact, and connection desired by baby boomers.

A Loving Lobby

These spaces give the first impression of a church to a boomer. Remember what the shampoo commercial says about first impressions: They set the tone for the whole experience. Is your lobby like an impersonal jail cell or a loving luxury hotel lobby? To improve the cheerfulness, human comfort, and connection, add friendly fellowship building forms. Take an expedition to several hotel lobbies to get a feel for their atmosphere. Remember, hotels are in the business of welcoming people. What are the seating accommodations like? How about natural lighting? Plants? The information sign-in centers? Do they have elegant outdoor drop-off areas? Hospitality centers? Are there waterfalls, fountains, sculptures, or fireplaces? After visiting several of these lobbies, travel into your church lobby with a critical eye. Is it like a hotel lobby or a jail cell? Obviously you cannot spend hundreds of thousands of dollars to match the aura of a Hilton or Sheraton Ritz. But let us examine what we can do for under three hundred dollars.

Top billing goes to the hospitality center. Basically, this is a table with linen, flowers, a coffee and/or a teapot, a server/greeter, and maybe some fresh fruit or breakfast cakes. Notice how the offer of a soothing drink and small pastries perks up everyone. A hospitality center brings out conversation in people. It also encourages the members to get to know visitors.

Comfortable fellowship area near lobby in Plymouth Congregational Church, Minneapolis, Minnesota.

Second billing goes to a relaxing seating arrangement. The church I grew up in had a parlor off of the room where the coffee was served. While we kids ran around, the adults seemed to talk forever. Today, many churches have developed this concept one step further. They place the sitting parlors or fireside rooms in the lobby for an even greater effect. These areas add the convenience and comfort required to boost fellowship.

If you do not have enough room for a loving lobby, create some additional space. Put up a fellowship tent in good weather. Do not waste God's gift of great weather by trapping people inside. A tent creates cool shade and a comfortable atmosphere to chat. Make it complete with chairs, coffee, and greenery. The atmosphere of the church will become like that of the circus days of old. Everyone will have fun under and around the old big top!

If none of the above is possible, then do the simple things that add some cheerfulness. Flowers, plants, colorful and informative bulletin boards, and some banners are all possible ways to enhance your lobby for less than three hundred dollars. But their usefulness is like money in the bank.

The main purpose of the church lobby is to encourage fellowship. We are called to "provoke one another to love and good deeds, not neglecting to meet together . . . but encouraging one another" (Hebrews 10:24-25). By encouraging comfortable contact between persons, the lobby is one of the best places to inspire "love and good deeds" in others.

A Nurturing Nursery

Baby boomers are finicky about the environment their children occupy. Dark church nurseries that have worn-out furnishings repel rather than attract young families. Boomers demand compliance. They will compare a church's nursery to the preschool center their children attend throughout the week. Therefore, create a modern, well-stocked nursery by using the following design ideas:

* Redecorate with new wallpaper, curtains, countertops, and changing tables.

Remodeled nursery at Bear Creek Presbyterian Church in Lakewood, Colorado, includes skylights and colorful wall mural.

* Restock with new toys and books—ones that will work, are safe, and will last. (Toys that are more than two years old are usually outdated and ready for the garbage pile.)
* Restaff with qualified, trained, and cheerful *paid* workers. (Incompetent volunteer staff members are hard to fire.)
* Install a bulletin board to announce special events, celebrate birthdays, introduce visitors, or congratulate graduates. Use colorful, simple shapes. Photographs capture and exhibit the special moments children experience in a nursery. Parents are impressed by the displays of their children's triumphs.

Bear Creek Presbyterian Church recognized the need to do some simple nursery modernizing. New paint, carpet, and countertops cheerfully enhanced their ministry to young families. Today it is one of the strengths of their ministry.

The Festival Center

When was the last time you had a festival, rather than just a worship service? Why are weddings so special and Sunday services so ordinary? Aim at having a festival time every week. All you need is superb planning and some decorations—not just banners here and there, but the type of decorations that make Christmas or a wedding so special. Flowers, trees, cloth sculptures, candles, children's drawings, special lights, dramatic costumes for performers and pastors, are some of the possibilities. In talking about the vines and the branches from John 15, the pastor might ask the congregation to bring in their house plants or trim some of their outdoor shrubs. If the theme is on Beatitudes, have the

Medieval scenery for a sanctuary festival at Mission Hills Baptist Church, Littleton, Colorado. Photograph by Mike Galius, Joy Photography.

children decorate and display posters on how each principle affects their lives.

A church in Denver produced a musical that depicted a medieval setting. They used painted plywood, colored mylar sheeting, and lights to create a perfect setting of false stained-glass windows and stone walls. The mood was set and the festival was perfect. People are still talking about it; they look forward to seeing the next idea that blossoms.

Old Testament festivals are a good example of celebrations to follow. They had all of the ingredients of a victory celebration—singing, dancing, feasting, and prayers. It was a time of great joy and thanksgiving. Is this similar to your worship services? Remember, boomers like cheerfulness, involvement, change, and contact with other people. They see effective worship as celebration, not just meditation. They are attracted to churches that make worship more like a festival than a funeral.

Spaces for Small Groups

When I go into my son's kindergarten classroom, I am amazed at what a fun place it looks like. Playful animals describe the alphabet and numbers. The morning class organizes contests and displays a scoreboard. Their school motto, "Peak Performance," hangs on one wall and a display of children characters translate the principles to five year olds. For some unheard of "fun" reason all their own, they have a footed bathtub. In short, that room is theirs. They "own" that room, and it expresses them. What a fun place in which to learn!

What do I see in my son's Sunday school classroom? Few enjoyable displays. Plain colored walls and movable partitions in a pale room. Nothing indicates that this is a church learning room for five year olds. No class title or display. No special props personalize the space. Which room do you think my son enjoys going to more? Which type of room should your church provide for all its small groups?

Kindergarten classroom in school is exciting, "fun" place to be.

Kindergarten classroom in church is dull, uninviting.

Decorate classrooms and activity centers with items for the people who occupy each room—bulletin boards, photos, artwork, and mementos. These personalize a room and honor those who use it. They also create cheerfulness and memories of the good times.

Keep memories up to date. A Nebraska church has a class for its senior members. When the teacher suggested that they move a twenty-year-old fake schefflera plant, half of the class nearly voted her out. How could they think of disgracing "Aunt Ruby," who had donated the object several years ago? Small groups need new memories, not worn out old ones. How about a photo display of all the great-great-grandchildren? Or a bulletin board telling how God is answering their prayers? Keep the periscope sights looking forward, as Paul did. He kept "pressing on" toward the "upward call of God" (see Phil. 3:12-16). Pressing backward attracts few participants!

A fresh coat of paint does miracles for a worn-out classroom. Let the occupants of each room choose the colors. Let them paint their class logo and name on the outside of the door. The project will bring people together and allow them to individualize their space. Many youth groups paint their classrooms, but adults and children can use this concept, too.

Facilities for the Disabled

The easiest way to help the disabled is to provide handicap parking. Make the spaces twelve feet wide, and provide enough spaces to equal at least 2 percent of your total number of parking stalls. If you have a higher need, add more spaces. Be sure to post the proper signs. If you need assistance, contact your local zoning department to answer questions on where these signs should be placed.

A wood ramping system is an inexpensive way of allowing wheelchair access to stepped entrances. The proper slope is one foot of length for every inch of height. Contact your local building department for the proper size of construction material. To improve the appearance, carefully integrate the materials of the ramp to match the building's architecture.

To provide wheelchair seating in fixed seating auditoriums, you might have a woodcrafter cut off a few feet of several pew ends. Provide as many three-foot-wide pew spaces as you have handicap parking spaces. Scatter these special spaces throughout the worship center, so that people in wheelchairs may sit with their families and not in a special place designated for wheelchairs.

Get Expert Advice

As churches examine themselves and the symptoms of their illnesses, they are often like doctors who try to perform surgery on themselves. They want the very best, but as they lie on their backs the pain from the scalpel is too great to make the surgical incision. For churches, some projects need the expertise and objectivity of an outside "doctor." Therefore, you sometimes need to get the opinion of an unbiased, outside expert—such as a landscape consultant for flowers, a preschool director for your nursery, an architect or interior designer for decorative solutions, a school teacher for youth rooms, and a local building department official for handicap access. Obviously, with a three hundred dollar limit, the advice will have to be *pro bono,* and therefore very general. But the wisdom will be invaluable.

> By wisdom a house is built,
>   and by understanding it is established;
> by knowledge the rooms are filled
>   with all precious and pleasant riches.
>   (Prov. 24:3-4)

Be wise, understanding, and knowledgeable in the use of the top twenty ideas for under three hundred dollars. They can build the house God desires, where living stones are brought into eternal relationship. Now we will look at these and other areas of potential improvement in greater detail.

III

AN EXALTING EXTERIOR

To begin the exercise of evaluating the first impressions your church's exterior makes, take a mental tour of your city. Locate several prominent funeral homes and church buildings. Imagine them during the warm months and cold months, daytime and night. After you obtain a mental picture, describe these two types of structures to a friend.

In many instances, you will hear yourself using the same adjectives to describe both churches and funeral homes—such as *stately, dignified, grand, subdued, respectful, traditional, somewhat boring, lifeless,* and *hard.* Is it any wonder that so many people do not go to church? Often their first impression of a church building classifies the worship experience in the same file as going to a funeral—a very difficult event. (In fact, most often the only time unchurched people enter either type of building is for a funeral.)

Yes, that comparison is unfair, shallow, and unspiritual. But our society has developed many stereotypical prejudices with regard to these types of buildings. A church body can be vibrant and alive in any type of setting. But if we want to eliminate the barriers that may hamper a ministry to all people, we will want to make our exteriors exalting.

Robert Bast, in his book *The Missing Generation,* recognizes our society's propensity to prejudge by first impressions. No matter how friendly and likable a person is, if that person does not shower he or she will have difficulty making new friends. Just as personal hygiene and style of hair and dress affect your initial reaction to an individual, so also the age, size, architectural style, and general grooming of a building play an important role in your impression of a church.[1]

For many congregations, the first step in improving first impressions is to move from a funeral home image to a God's home image. The following ideas can help church leaders begin that process.

1. Maintenance. Many people believe that "a cluttered desk means a cluttered mind." So too a shabby exterior gives the impression of a shabby service. Boomers are "committed to excellence at work and are turned off by shabbiness that characterizes many local churches."[2] Shabbiness offends God if it blocks a church from getting attention in a positive way.

Ecclesiastes 10:18 states that the owners of a dumpy house are lazy. Proverbs 24:30-31 describes the field of a sluggard as being weed infested. Does this describe your grounds? Is the landscaping well kept? Does the sign advertise the correct time of services in a well maintained fashion? Does the exterior have a fresh coat of paint? Is the fence in good repair? Are the outdoor equipment and trash dumpsters hidden from view? Are the outside lights half burned out? The little things add up to create a properly maintained structure. Cleaning and making repairs are just as important as brushing your teeth and combing your hair. A church should allocate at least 5 percent of its budget to maintenance projects.

2. Openness. Visitors to a church are looking for two traits in a church body: warmth and accessibility. Communicate these traits in architectural terms by being welcoming versus fortress-like, comfortable versus hard, warm versus cold, easy to understand versus confusing, accepting versus restrictive. On which side of these scales is your structure?

Begin with the landscaping if you want to soften and warm a cold structure. Landscape at least 20 percent of the church grounds. Pay particular attention to spots that have the greatest visibility and human contact. Make areas around the sign, the entrance doors, and the parking lot entrances priorities for landscaping touches. The famous American architect Frank Lloyd Wright once said, "Doctors get to bury their mistakes. Architects have to plant vines." If your architecture has a deadly appearance, then plant something—anything—that is attractive, colorful, and concealing.

Entry areas are especially critical. Many churches unconsciously project a historic motif that seems to isolate people from God. Thick, fortress-like stone walls that are raised on a pedestal approached by numerous steps, and imposing wooden doors with massive hardware all contribute to a medieval atmosphere. People today desire contemporary styles and comfort from their God, and from their church entry areas as well.

Try softening the entrance areas with some colorful awnings or banners. A fountain also creates a soothing and reflective atmosphere. A terrace and entry that extend the lobby to the outside have also been successful at a few churches, like the Lutheran Church in downtown Boulder, Colorado. These churches have added on to their lobby spaces in order to humanize their exterior architecture (see chap. 4). Anything that conveys a park-like setting attracts boomers and everyone to your front door.

3. Identity. One of Dave's top ten tips for starting a business is, "Create a distinctive image so the customer won't forget you."[3] Dave Thomas is famous for the restaurant chain he named after his daughter, Wendy. His 3,800 restaurants worldwide reinforce the value of his advice that any business and/or church must have a clear and positive identity. Even without the name, millions of people recognize the red mansard roofs with the picture of a pigtailed girl.

A church's identity becomes especially important when we remember that a large percentage of newcomers who join a church attend the first time because they noticed the church when traveling in the neighborhood. If people notice a church and like what they see, many of them will visit. A

Large banners designed by artist Lehlan Murray soften the Gothic exterior of St. John's Episcopal Cathedral in Denver.

church's identity is established through two equal elements: signs and architecture.

Significant Signs

This is the number-one way to build image. It is also one of the most important types of church advertising. The key factors to quality signs include the following.

Place signs perpendicular to the road. Four times as many people see a sign that is perpendicular to the street, compared to signs parallel to it.

Keep the sign simple. Large, simple, and legible letters should incorporate only the name of your church and the time of the services. All other information will clutter the readability. Match materials to your building's architecture—that is, a stucco building demands a stucco sign with

33

fiber glass letters. The height in inches of the letters in a church's name should be at least 0.21 times the speed of cars that travel the street. For example, if cars routinely travel 40 MPH past a church sign, then the height of the letters should be 8.4 or 8.5 inches tall. The letters for the schedule can be one-half to one-third the size of the name.

Raise the sign above the interference. A nicely designed sign that is obstructed by parked cars or landscaping is useless. Check with local zoning ordinances as you plan to raise the sign above the obstructions. But a person traveling at 30 MPH needs 310 feet of sight line to provide the distance needed to read the lettering; 60 MPH needs 610 feet of unobstructed visibility. As much as possible, try to remove the sight line clutter at an appropriate distance.

Drop denominational barriers from the name. Baby boomers have little loyalty to denominational titles. (Some of them may even be hostile to some denominations.) Therefore, several churches have decided to remove the denominational title from their church name. The Wooddale Baptist Church in Minneapolis became Wooddale Church. The Central Community Church of God, in Wichita, Kansas, became Central Community Church (but only on its sign; it left the denominational tag on its legal documents). The Van Nuys Foursquare Church in Van Nuys, California, changed its name to The Church on the Way.

Display the church logo. People are attracted by images of people. The Girl Scouts incorporate the face of a young woman in their logo. The Denver Dumb Friends League features a small child and pet dog. Because churches are made up of people, develop a church logo that includes people and incorporate it into the church sign. Again, the logo for Wendy's displays a cute, innocent, pigtailed, red-haired girl, and McDonald's uses a happy clown named Ronald.

Attractive Architecture

When Willow Creek Community Church began developing its 120 acres in the Chicago suburb of South Barrington,

Covered entry added to Grace Church in Edina, Minnesota, adds a contemporary feel to the 1940s structure.

the congregation wanted to project the image of a progressive civic center or college campus, one that was comfortable and nonthreatening for their unchurched neighbors.

When Oglethorpe Mall in Savannah, Georgia, began to be challenged by a new mall in their town, they decided to create a more 1990s look. The subsequent remodeling removed the aged 1960s look. New entrances with bright colors and archways replaced the fortress architecture. They also added night lighting to increase the sparkle of their image at night. The cosmetic surgery was remarkable. Before and after photographs show two entirely different structures. The architect created the unique and positive identity David Thomas calls for; yet, the costs were minimal.

Sometimes the older structures can be updated with simple additions. Grace Church in Edina, Minnesota, is an example of how simple architectural additions can bring a facelift to a 1940s structure. The new two-story steeple and skylight covered entry is described as a "new architectural statement for a new decade" in a church brochure. The minor addition is big enough to be seen by passing motorists on France Avenue, yet modern enough to contrast sharply with boring 1940s architectural dogma.

Sometimes, the remodeling of the exterior can be combined with internal requirements. Grace Lutheran Church in Boulder, Colorado, combined the need for an enlarged lobby with the desire to modernize its image. The subsequent stone and large glass windows matched the historic character but gave comfort and warmth to the imposing structure. Other churches have combined handicap accessibility with exterior updates. Nursery relocation, restroom enlargement, or office additions are all ways to improve a church's identity.

Funeral homes and dated church structures conjure up similar images to many Americans—sad and boring experiences that few people enjoy. Contrast these feelings to the excitement and anticipation of the psalmist when his friends suggested going to the "house of the Lord." His heart pounded and his face brightened. To him it was heaven on earth (Ps. 122:1). Does your church's exterior create this type of excitement and anticipation?

IV

PRECIOUS PARKING

The automobile industry pays billions of dollars to advertising experts so that we will fall in love with their cars. We are exposed numerous times to their slick autos racing across swervy roads each year. For what? In order to make that automobile *our* god.

The advertisers—to a large extent—have succeeded. We love our wheels. Bright, shiny, and pampered, they dominate much of our lives. But just as our cars have gone beyond mere transportation, so also our standards for what a parking lot should be have risen beyond bare dirt. Here are some minimum standards, which if not met by the church will mean failure to reach many people who drive cars to worship services.

1. Off-street parking can be very expensive. But if you think land prices are high, consider the cost of the alternative: a limited congregation size. People will not attend churches where they cannot find a parking spot. If the average family in your church gives about $2,000 a year, you lose $2,000 per year for every parking stall you need but do not have.

For churches in older locations, insufficient parking is the top membership growth hindrance. The proper parking ratio is one space for every two morning worshipers (figure the average annual attendance at the largest service, if you have more than one). Therefore, parking is the first place to spend funds.

One option to the high cost of land is a parking garage. Unfortunately, parking structures are also costly. But even at an average cost of $7,800 per parking stall, a parking garage breaks even at about the fourth year for the average congregation. Some churches that consider this alternative decide to move rather than fight the problem. Relocating may be wise in some instances, but it may be far more expensive than building a parking garage.

2. Paved parking can also be expensive, but it is a requirement in most municipalities. People expect the same conveniences at church as they receive at work and school. No one likes to walk in the muck of a muddy parking area—especially in Sunday clothes and polished shoes. So the church parking lot that conforms to people's expectations will also attract newcomers and help to keep the regulars.

Paving thickness designs vary greatly, so consult with several paving contractors in your area to determine what performs best in your soil conditions. Asphalt and concrete are the two basic surface materials, but the amount of rock or base course under the pavement is also a key factor. Other important design characteristics are:

The slope of the ground. Between 1 percent and 7 percent (6 percent for ice and snow conditions) slope is ideal. A slope of less than 1 percent creates water puddling that causes premature aging of the pavement and requires greater maintenance. Steeper slopes make traction difficult and walking hazardous in icy conditions. To alleviate problems on a hilly site try terracing the parking into flatter areas.

Concrete curbs or wheel stops. These accessories keep cars from damaging landscaping. They also protect pedestrians on adjacent walks and curbs with landscaping. Curbs with gutters collect water before it runs under paving, where it may cause damage. Drive into school and work parking lots to see the local standards.

Striping. Stripes increase parking efficiency and help to prevent car doors from dinging their neighbor's auto. All municipalities have minimum parking stall dimensions. Call the local planning/zoning offices and ask for your community's standard dimensions. They may also allow compact parking stalls. Ask for the allowable ratio of regular to compact and the size of compact spaces. But never go below eight feet six inches in width or less than fifteen feet in length.

Angled parking should also be considered, because it facilitates easier traffic flow. This is why so many shopping centers utilize angled parking. They willingly increase the asphalt area by 10 to 20 percent in order to increase customer satisfaction by the same amount. To find the design standards in your area, contact your local planning/zoning office.

Rainwater detention. When an unpaved area becomes paved the rain that would have been absorbed into the ground becomes runoff. This runoff can contribute to massive flooding downstream if the water is not detained and released at a natural rate. Most municipalities have very strict rules on how big to make the detention area, where it can be located, and the rate the water is released. A local municipality's engineering department will answer the question of whether water detention is needed. If it is, a civil engineer will have to do the calculations and design.

3. Directional signage reduces disorder. Why do fast food restaurants use directional signage? The clarity reduces the confusion. This makes for happy customers and greater customer loyalty.

For a church the scenario is similar. Their lot has highly concentrated use in a relatively short time frame. In some cases hundreds of cars are trying to enter and park within fifteen to twenty minutes. To a visitor the rush could be frustrating and confusing. In order to ease the discomfort, many churches install directional signs. Try to answer the following questions: Where do people enter and exit? Where is additional parking located? Visitor parking? If there is a side street access, erect a sign that states the church's name and has an arrow that gives directions. For many churches, the main door and drop off is obscure. By helping people locate the entrance, you eliminate a hassle for visitors.

4. Scrape snow clean. In snowy climates, nothing decreases church attendance better than a few snowflakes. But do not let the damp weather water down the spirit. Keep the pavement clean and the sidewalks dry. This will keep financial giving up and more than pay for the cost of snow removal. On the spiritual side of the equation, clear sidewalks help to keep a ministry united and moving ahead by reducing the loss of key commitment Sundays to bad weather and low attendance.

5. Protect parishioners with parking lot lighting. At night, safety is directly correlated to visibility. If a church offers evening activities, then safety lighting is a necessity. One-half foot-candle of light coverage is the minimum light level for security. To achieve this level, an electrical engineer will design a combination of fixture height, location, and wattage. Careful design standards keep light from glaring into a church's neighboring residential windows.

Some dedicated church leaders may respond to these suggestions by saying, "All of these parking elements seem excessive. Why not let people walk farther from on-street parking spots or take a church bus?" The best answer to that question is another question: Why not let people use outdoor plumbing? Because parking and plumbing are equally commanded—not by God, but by the people. And we do not want to place roadblocks in front of God's ministry. When Jesus entered Jerusalem on Palm Sunday, he was riding a very special donkey—not because it was fast, or strong, but because God had chosen it. The most effective churches treat each family's "donkey" as if it were carrying Jesus, giving it the utmost pampering and respect—not because cars are biblical, but because the provisions churches make for them help to accomplish God's purposes in the lives of God's people.

V

A ROYAL LOBBY

When looking at your entry area(s), put yourself in the shoes of two different people.

Imagine being the Prince of Wales. You are entering the grand cathedral, St. Paul's in London. The ceremony is a victory service to thank God for protection during a long war. As you enter the front doors, you see a red carpet. Colorfully dressed guards direct you to the proper location. The live orchestra plays Handel's "Messiah" to set the mood for worship. Several church leaders greet you with a warm handshake and a broad smile. The building is decorated with the bright colors of the season, and the lights are turned up for this festive occasion. If you have a coat or need to use the restroom, the facilities are convenient, probably polished and newly painted. If you are early you will be guided to a comfortable seat where you will chat with your entourage.

Now imagine being a very nondescript first-time visitor to Average Church, U.S.A. You may not want the notoriety of Prince Charles, but you would appreciate being treated like a king. Unfortunately, visitors who enter many church buildings are greeted by a long dark hallway and uncaring strangers. What do you do? Where do you go? Where is the restroom? Or the nursery? Why should you return?

Many visitors ask themselves these questions at Average Church, U.S.A. The way the building and the members answer these questions explains why only 15 percent of first-time visitors return and eventually join an average church. For many visitors, the first impression is uncomfortable, sometimes even hostile.

The good news: Some churches have been able to increase their odds. They realize what several church consultants express: First-time visitors to a church decide if they want to return within the first ten to fifteen minutes of entering the property. Therefore, a quality drop off and lobby is an important factor in encouraging people to return. With quality programs and spaces, some churches have been able to retain up to 30 percent, and a few as high as 40 percent, of their visitors.

What is the secret? *Treat everyone like royalty.* Why? Because God says they are. Romans 8:15-17 has profound implications for our ministries and facilities. As children of the King, we deserve the best—the best teaching, training, support, and even lobby space.

1. Royalty deserves comfort. The lobby should be one-third the size of the sanctuary. The number-one building complaint of senior pastors is expressed most often as: "Our lobby is like a cattle chute where people are herded back and forth between classes and the auditorium." Too many churches have a thousand-seat sanctuary but only a twenty-foot-square lobby space. There is no place for greetings, conversation, or relaxing. People feel shoved and pushed, as if they were entering an outdated baseball stadium during the playoffs.

Create some space for lounging. Trinity Lutheran Church in Boulder, Colorado, extended its lobby just twenty feet. But connected to the three hundred-seat sanctuary, this enlarged lobby created the space and ambience needed for comfort. With large windows, seating areas, plants, and nicely carpeted areas the church is a delight to enter.

If you cannot add interior space, consider an exterior patio or garden. During moderate weather these spaces can be glorious. An example is Lakewood United Church of Christ

Quality lobby space provides seating areas, information counter, and chandelier lighting.

in Lakewood, Colorado, where the sweet aroma of flowering trees and shrubs, the sounds of cheerfully singing birds, and comfortable seating encourage parishioners to mingle before and after services.

Add intimate appeal. A church lobby should not feel like an airport terminal, where people rush through to get someplace else. Church lobbies are places for human contact and communication, places that combat loneliness. Add plants, water amenities, seats, a fireplace, and carpet—creating a place for greeters and minglers to extend a warm handshake and a hug. Grace Church, Edina, Minnesota, is a leader in lobby design. Not just because its leaders converted the old sanctuary into a huge lobby, but because they understand that quality is as important as quantity. Wide-open spaces are great for basketball, but people at Grace Church want to be less conspicuous after a worship service. So they created a luxurious hotel lobby appeal.

Make the church accessible to all. Quality involves more than handicap accessibility (see chapter 10). Accessibility means a central access point, like the hub of a wheel—a place that eliminates confusion by being directly accessible to nursery, restrooms, offices, sanctuary, and coat racks. The antithesis of this idea is a church building I visited in Nebraska. It has so many entrances down dark corridors that visitors often feel as if they are entering the Roman Catacombs, not a house of God. After a service ends, the church becomes a stabbing victim as parishioners bleed out the numerous entrances. Members have no further opportunity to connect with each other, much less extend greetings to visitors. To correct this situation, the church plans to expand its corridor-like lobby and create a central location to help visitors and members alike. It will also add an elevator for persons with handicapping conditions and brighten the access points to the lower and upper levels.

Provide popular restrooms. When traveling by automobile, many people purchase gasoline only from certain outlets—not because of the quality or price of the fuel, but solely because of the condition of the restrooms. Church restrooms that are private, modern, clean, well-lit, and provide hot water, soap, paper products, and plenty of mirrors and counter space impress baby boomers. If your restrooms are more than than ten years old, then remodeling will produce improved ministry effects. This may be as simple as a coat of paint or as complicated as expansion and replumbing of fixtures.

2. Royalty desires rejoicing. The lobby is the prelude to the worship service. Therefore, set the tone. Encourage an uplifting mood. Provide natural lighting, a lighted ceiling, high ceiling area, and a spacious feeling that fulfills the psalm, "Enter his gates with thanksgiving,/ and his courts with praise" (Ps. 100:4).

Counter the Sunday blues as did St. James Presbyterian, Littleton, Colorado. That congregation expanded its church to include a marvelous lobby. It offers brilliant sunshine and

Lobby of St. James Presbyterian Church in Littleton, Colorado, is bright, cheerful, and can comfortably accommodate a large number of people.

peaked volumes to introduce a worshiper to the festive services.

3. Royalty demands involvement. God condemns faith without works (James 2:14-26). Therefore, a church is responsible to show people how they can be involved—as a Bible study teacher, as a fellowship group leader, by inviting a neighbor to the Christmas concert, as a youth club volunteer, or by baking cookies for elderly shut-ins. All churches need a place to show off their ministries to get people excited with banners, information packets, bulletin boards, and sign-up tables. The lobby is the place to display the opportunities. At Calvary Chapel in Littleton, Colorado, the displays are complete, orderly, colorful, and profession-al. They have catchy slogans and exciting graphics. Last and most important, they are changed every couple of months. Thus they remain fresh and relevant.

4. Royalty also demands improvement. One of the best places for self-improvement is a church library. And the best place for a library is off the lobby. If your pastor speaks on financial accountability and supplements the thirty-minute sermon with a five-book reference list and all the books are available in the church library, the sermon's impact enlarges considerably.

Baby boomers want to improve themselves. Therefore, they will seek self-help books—books that teach relevant application on subjects such as prayer, God's will, spiritual conflicts, human relationships, family, marriage, personality types, and so on.

To encourage use, libraries desire the real estate motto, "location, location, and location." The best location is connected to the main circulation focus, or the lobby. When Hope Presbyterian Church in Richfield, Minnesota, opens the huge sliding glass doors to the library, it becomes part of the lobby. People browse as if they were in a bookstore at a shopping mall. And the products are displayed in a similar fashion for maximum use.

If space is a problem, then a small cart or a table of books is a good alternative—like Redlands Community Church in Grand Junction, Colorado. They use a scaled-down version of the bookstore concept, where they key in on certain relevant subjects that are tied to the sermons.

Greater Contact Produces Increased Involvement

The retail industry has a relevant sales philosophy: The longer people stay, the more they will buy. This philosophy is carried to the extreme at Byerly's of Minneapolis. They have transformed a huge grocery store into a huge and luxurious grocery store. In so doing they have proven the theory that the more you like the atmosphere, the longer you will stay; the longer you stay, the more you will purchase.

Churches are for giving rather than for selling, but a similar theory applies: The more people like the atmosphere, the longer they will stay. The more the contact with other laity, the greater their involvement and commitment. This process starts with a royal lobby. A quality lobby encourages contact between people and is the inverse of the old saying, "Bad company corrupts good character" (see 1 Cor. 15:33).

Well-designed lobbies help to transform that maxim into "Good company builds godly character." The longer visitors and regulars stay, the better they can become. Providing spaces that encourage contact between church people is more than an architectural project; it is a fellowship-spiritual growth builder.

VI

A NURTURING NURSERY

Close behind precious parking and royal lobby—but ahead of sanctuary, classrooms, and office—comes the nurturing nursery. Before spending a dime on any area used by adults, check out the children's corner. Give this area the highest priority for three reasons:

1. A parent may be thrilled with a church's music, gripped by the pastor's preaching, embraced by dozens of parishioners, and supported by a caring staff, but a negative evaluation of just one aspect of the nursery's quality can erase all of these positives. Baby boomers demand the best for their babies—the best clothes, the best toys, the best education, and the best nursery spaces. Show me a church that is growing, and I will show you a church that has a fine nursery.

2. Baby boomers have high expectations. Since most baby boomer parents work, many place their children in weekday child-care centers. This billion-dollar industry is designed to produce quality. Parents hire these professionals to pamper, please, and parent their children. What happens when these same parents visit churches and find the opposite circumstances—cramped quarters, worn-out toys, overtaxed and undertrained staff? A room full of preschoolers is a room full of opportunities for shaping a church's future.

3. Christ commands us to be kind to children, showing compassion and encouraging them to find Jesus (Matthew 18 and 19).

The church's goal should be to fulfill the requirements for a licensed child-care center. Contact your state department of social services and obtain a copy of their regulations. Then visit several quality programs to see the activities and the design of their structure. Spend the funds needed to mimic their ideas. Skimping on the nursery area creates a skimpy ministry to young families.

Evaluate your ministry to nursery residents and their parents by reviewing the following items:

1. Location, location, location. These are the top three rules for designing a nursery space. A superior location is off the lobby. If this is not possible, locate the nursery on the same level as the sanctuary, no more than fifty feet from the lobby. Parents like their children to be close and safe. They also have difficulty in carrying small children with a blanket and diaper bag down the hall, up the stairs, and two turns to the right in heavy traffic. Arriving late with a child who is teething compounds the frustration.

2. No parents allowed. Because of security and sanitation, allow only staff to enter the nursery. This means you need a drop-off counter to create a separation between public and private areas. This area is also helpful in exchanging the children and accessories, and the removal of cold weather garments. If designed properly, the drop-off counter can also be used as a diaper-changing counter and a storage location for toys, diaper bags, and coats. (A storage compartment for each child facilitates easy access and coordination.)

When designing a diaper-changing counter, safety and cleanliness are the watchwords. For safety, it needs a surrounding curb to prevent children from rolling off. Cleanliness means it is made of plastic laminate with a plastic covered mat for easy wipe down with a disinfectant solution. Also, provide supply storage within easy reach and a sink to wash hands before and after each changing. Last, provide a place to dispose of dirty diapers.

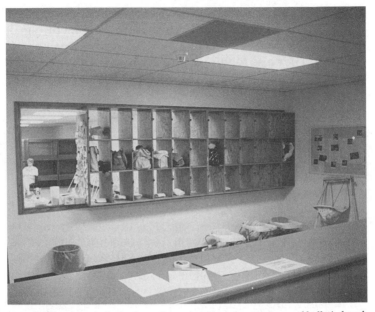

Remodeled nursery includes drop-off counter, diaper bag storage, and bulletin board.

In the nursery design of Mission Hills Baptist Church, in Littleton, Colorado, safety and security were given highest priority. The people even padded the carpet to ensure that little mishaps do not become major tragedies.

3. Spacious space. Nursery areas were once designed from leftovers—a leftover storage area or classroom corner. Not today. Nursery areas demand prime real estate. Twenty-five to thirty square feet per child is the requirement. The area is often segmented into places for children to sleep, a place for children unable to walk, a place for walkers, and a place for nursing mothers to have some privacy. There should be at least one toilet and sink, and a place to store a vacuum cleaner. Some churches also desire a kitchen area to warm bottles and store snacks, and a location to launder sheets and sterilize toys. These spacious accommodations seem generous—until you fill them with rocking chairs, swings, toys, and the large staff needed for this specialized age group.

In Colorado, licensed child-care centers are required to

allocate space for separate play areas. Art supplies, blocks, books, and dramatic play, large muscle equipment, small manipulative toys, musical toys, and science materials are all required. They also require seventy-five feet of outdoor areas for each of the children who may occupy the play area at the same time. The outdoor area must be surrounded by walls, a fence, or a hedge to keep children safe.

4. Environment amenities. Besides sheer volume of space, nurturing nurseries require minimum environmental standards. Cleanliness, good ventilation, and seventy-two degrees at the floor level are musts. But so are carpeting (a short, closed loop that is stain resistant and fire retardant), natural light from skylights or windows, cheerfully coordinated colors, soundproofing, and direct access to an outdoor play area for the older children. The soundproofing should be at least an extra layer of 5/8-inch-thick drywall or a layer of three-inch-thick sound insulation in the walls. (The outdoor play area standards can be obtained from your local social services regulations.) The last two items may be considered luxuries by leaders in some churches. Others, who see their ministry to young families as priority number one, will find a way to include them.

5. Numbering system. If a church plans on ministering to more than fifteen children in the nursery, it needs a numbering system. This keeps track of who the children and parents are, which accessories belong to each child, where the parents will be, and how to notify them if they are needed. Upon drop off, a small number is pinned on the child's clothing, and a duplicate is given to the parent. The diaper bag, blanket, coat, or whatever the parent has brought with the child is placed in a numbered compartment. The parent fills out an information sheet, telling the staff about special needs or schedule of the child and indicates where the parent(s) will be during their time at church. If there is a need for parental assistance, the staff can locate the parent(s). Some churches use a visual pager system, mounted in full view in the worship center, to notify parents if they are needed in the nursery. (You may obtain information on a system by calling the Microframe Corporation, 1-800-635-3811.) The numbering system provides protection by allowing only the parent with the number to pick up the child. This limits the risk of a stranger or an unsupervised sibling from snatching a child. This may seem excessive security, but infants are occasionally stolen from hospitals and day-care centers.

6. Cry room. Many parents with very young children desire to spend their church time with their youngsters. Weekday separation or a minor crisis or the need to be breast fed are some of the reasons. But the parents also desire to be in the church service. This requires a private viewing location, or cry room. These areas are always placed at the rear of a worship center, but adjacent to the nursery. Soundproofing, one-way mirrored glass, rocking chairs, and a separate sound system are essential. Twenty square feet per parent/child is appropriate.

This whole chapter has emphasized one objective: baby pampering. Why is this so important for churches? Because it is a principle held dear by all members of our society. The concept has become so prevalent that the managers of a shopping mall in Denver are going the extra mile to attract young parents by giving away free disposable diapers, stroller rentals, and toddler snacks. In all the restrooms they have installed special diaper-changing counters. They call it their "Baby Your Baby" campaign. The marketing manager for the mall said, "The idea is to get them [the shoppers] spoiled here."

Several churches are also baby pampering—First Baptist in Watsonville, California; Bear Creek Presbyterian in Denver; Bethany Church in Long Beach, California; Bible Baptist in Astoria, Oregon; and Salem Heights Church in Salem, Oregon—all have created nurturing nursery spaces recently. The response from baby boomer parents has been tremendous.

VII

A CELEBRATION CENTER

Parking, the lobby, and the nursery are important dishes in the cafeteria of items that make church facilities effective. But the worship center is the "meat and potatoes" of a parishioner's experience. It is the main course that 85 percent of worship visitors rank high on the list of meaningful factors in a church building.

What kind of food do baby boomers want? What kind of facilities do they want it served on?

1. A place to meet God (worship).
2. A place to be challenged (teaching).
3. A place to be family (acceptance).
4. A place that is creative (variety).

Preferences have changed from past generations. Preaching was the number-one priority of worshipers until about 1980. Today, worship and teaching (not preaching) each share about 35 percent of people's worship preference plate. Acceptance is the vegetable, at 20 percent, and variety is the garnish at 10 percent. Together, this quartet sums up the expectations of today's worshipers.

Worship: A Place to Meet God

We do not need great buildings to meet God. Many people meet God on the streets of our inner cities or in the countryside. "Draw near to God, and he will draw near to you" (James 4:8). But we are "surroundings sensitive." A great worship center can inspire us to move in God's direction. "One thing I asked of the LORD . . . to live in the house of the LORD all the days of my life . . . to inquire in his temple" (Ps. 27:4).

Worship inspiration develops through two dimensions. The first and foremost is *music*. The worshiper is nurtured, healed and redirected by the process of worship, and the music plays a major role in that process. According to Elmer Towns, churches that attract large numbers of young adults tailor their music to the preferences of their people.[4] Some examples are:

*Perimeter Church in Atlanta was custom fitting the music when it switched to praise choruses.
*Central Community in Wichita, Kansas, uses a wide range of music from Bach to rock.
*Willow Creek in South Barrington, Illinois, has a "seeker service" with contemporary Christian music.
*The Church on the Way in Van Nuys, California, uses choruses and old hymns to develop "intimacy between the worshiper and God," according to Pastor Jack Hayford, Jr.

Each of these churches seems intent on encouraging people by song. They use a combination of easy to sing rhythmic songs; complicated, but familiar, traditional songs that everyone wants to sing; and sophisticated choir songs that are felt in the soul. Most of these churches have limited the amount of organ music they use and have added an orchestra or band to increase emotion and tempo.

These changes toward contemporary music have a dynamic impact on facility designs. The songs are often projected on large screens. The platform requires sufficient space and flexibility to accommodate various sizes of vocal and instrumental groups. The acoustics are transformed from high church with long echoes to contemporary music with short, recognizable sounds. To understand the words, a reverberation time of about 1.7 seconds is desired (the amount of time a noise bounces around a room). To shorten reverberation time, add sound-absorbing materials, like soft banners hung from the ceiling or attached to walls. For a good source of design ideas, see "Acoustic Wall Hangings," an article on acoustical wall hangings by David McCandless.[5] Or add carpet to the floor or back of the auditorium wall. To lengthen reverberation time, add hard surfaces at different angles to the ceiling or walls. This can be done with wall board or wood surfaces.

Your church might play with the acoustics by itself, but hiring an acoustical engineer is recommended. Poor room acoustics can never be fixed by changing the PA system. The only way to solve room acoustics is to create new room acoustics.

The second dynamic that inspires worship is strictly cosmetic, the *architecture*. What should the worship center look like? Roman Catholics desire "a sense of something special in everything that is seen and heard, touched and smelled, and tasted in liturgy (or worship)."[6] The Southern Baptists state that "the environment has significant power over our emotions. Therefore, the places where we gather for worship should make positive, uplifting contributions to life-changing experiences." In short, it should be a place "that invites and enhances celebration."[7] No matter where churches are on the worship spectrum, they all desire the architecture to be worshipful.

For the baby boomer, worship architecture has come full circle. The pendulum has swung back to the "practice of early Christian times when priests and people gathered around the altar together to celebrate the eucharist."[8] The people want the spotlight turned off and the house lights turned up.

A "turned-up" sanctuary is, first, cheerful, bright, airy, and congregation focused versus mysterious, oppressive, heavy, and altar focused. Lightening up the colors and adding more natural and/or artificial light is like retuning your television. By adjusting the brightness and contrast buttons, the worship picture is clearer and sharper—tuned in to God.

Second, a turned-up sanctuary displays simplicity and purity, and it is expressive and relaxed versus cluttered, distracting, formal, and religious. Remove the religious makeup. By "cold creaming" most of the symbolism and focusing on fewer icons, worship will be more natural, focused, and honest.

The following examples of churches that remodeled in this way are mostly from historical mainline denominations. But most post-World War II church buildings need similar updating.

*Cathedral of Incarnation, Nashville, Tennessee
—Replaced dark-colored clerestory glass windows with clear beveled glass to add natural, sparkling light.
—Brightened lighting, interior paint, and flooring.
—Removed or relocated ornate decorations and paintings.
*St. Mary's Chapel, St. Paul, Minnesota
—Sandblasted ceiling to remove dark wood stain to reveal a rich and natural color.
—Removed trappings of religion, including choir stalls, symbolic wood paneling, and paraphernalia from stone columns.
*St. John's Church, Albany, New York
—Added dramatic up-lighting to express the structure and remove harsh glare.
*St. Thomas Aquinas, Boston, Massachusetts
—Repainted with pure white.
—Added lighting to promote participation.
*Hope Community Church, Chino, California
—Cleaned dirt from a cheap western look to see "contempo" California.
—Brown, cream, and gold colors were replaced by steel blue, mauve, and white.
—Removed wagonwheel lights.

Cathedral of the Incarnation in Nashville, Tennessee, before remodeling.

Cathedral after remodeling shows new lighting, removal of some religious ornamentation. Photos by Rion Rizzo, Creative Sources Photography, Atlanta, Georgia.

*Trinity Baptist Church, Wheat Ridge, Colorado
—Covered oppressive dark paneling with white drywall.
—Hung simple drywall "halo" over platform with recessed lights.
—Boosted light levels.
*St. Clement's Church, Chicago, Illinois
—Renovated the seventy-year-old Byzantine structure by increasing lighting levels through indirect up-lighting. This also illuminated the richly restored painting and mosaics on the ceiling.
*Cathedral Church of St. Paul, Boston, Massachusetts
—Renovated the 1820 Greek Revival building because of a less liturgical worship style.
—Repainted with bright rich combination of colors to accentuate coffered ceiling.

Teaching: A Place to Be Challenged

In changing their emphasis from preaching to teaching, contemporary churches accomplish a biblical imperative: "Let the word of Christ dwell in you richly; teach and admonish one another in all wisdom" (Col. 3:16).

The new approach changes leaders from masters to brothers—from kings to shepherds. Baby boomers distrust authority and despise orders. Instead, they welcome advice and wisdom. Pastor Ray Cotton of Central Community Church, Wichita, Kansas, states that he "has stopped preaching and begun speaking to people. I'm not giving orders (i.e., General George Patton) but talking with friends."[9] Pastor Bill Hybels of Willow Creek Community Church surveyed hundreds of unchurched people to find out why they avoid church. One reason: Preachers talk down to people. So Hybels counsels preachers on how to improve themselves by cultivating:

—honest personality
—personal examples
—effective and challenging application
—relevant biblical truth

An effective teaching environment includes:

Relaxed atmosphere. Expose the speaker to the audience without wall-like pulpit and with a wireless microphone. Second Baptist, Houston, uses comfortable den furniture to decorate the platform. Fellowship Community Church, Aurora, Colorado, creates a realistic fireplace and Christmas scene once a year. Most churches use greenery or flowers to loosen life.

Audible acoustics. Acoustics can turn the greatest sermon into a faint murmur or a brash clatter. Audible speaking creates distinct, precise language. To attain good room acoustics, you need (1) a public address system (a prerequisite); (2) a control board within the worship space and a qualified operator; (3) a properly adjusted equalizer and possibly a feedback stabilizer to compensate for room variables; (4) a speaker system tuned to give full coverage from above the platform; (5) quality microphones for the proper application and location; (6) two dual cassette decks for recording and playing; and (7) special monitors to play music for vocalists and other instrumentalists. Acoustic engineers are advised to design the best system.

Intimacy. Intimacy is directly related to proximity. Short, direct distances from speaker to congregation and low-height (eighteen inches maximum) platforms give direct eye contact. Remember the battle cry, "Do not fire until you see the whites of their eyes." The same formula achieves intimate auditoriums.

St. Thomas More Church, Braintree, Massachusetts, and Calbury Baptist Church, Montevideo, Minnesota, made intimacy their number-one priority. They reoriented the sanctuary from a long, narrow nave to short, wide radial seating. The dramatic change promotes heart to heart sermons.

Intimacy is also related to accessibility. Remove the barrier furniture. Cathedral of the Incarnation, in Nashville, removed "a communion rail that was perceived as a fence separating the priest from the parishioners."[10] St. Margaret's Episcopal Church in Washington, D.C., made its altar railing

St. Thomas More Church in Braintree, Massachusetts, before remodeling.

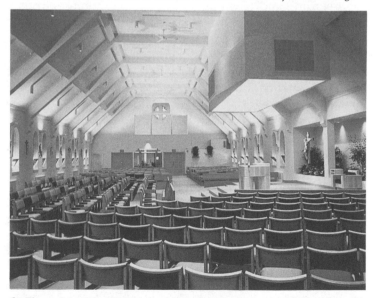

St. Thomas More Church after remodeling shows flexible seating, closer to the pulpit. Photographs by Betsy Nelson, De Castro/Nelson Assoc.

removable (for occasional use) and thrust its communion table into the audience.

Jesus taught in this type of atmosphere. With people gathered around, he taught from a hillside meadow (Matthew 5). Or they stood on the beach as he sat in a boat and broadcast over the water (Matthew 13). You see Jesus teaching in everyday settings at the Temple, in a wheat field, or in someone's house. He did not formally assemble his followers into a rigid teaching environment. Always, we see a relaxed and friendly setting.

Several old historic cathedrals have created a more intimate chancel with smaller pulpits, lecterns, and altars. They have moved the chancel closer to the people and eliminated or began using removable railings. Cathedral Church of St. Paul in Boston, St. Mary's Chapel in St. Paul, and St. Clements Church in Chicago are all beautiful, historic structures that demonstrate sensitive historic renovation within intimate atmospheres.

Acceptance: A Place to Be Family

Genuine love is commanded by God. "Let us work for the good of all, and especially for those of the family of faith" (Gal. 6:10). "Therefore encourage one another and build up each other" (1 Thess. 5:11).

But love is also a deep human craving. "People look for the worship services that communicate a warm, family feeling," states Herb Miller.[11] A church that serves up heaping helpings of brotherly love will have a long chow line.

What does a loving family atmosphere look like? A warm handshake. A gentle hug. A broad smile. A tearful embrace. A jolly chuckle. An accepting conversation. A concerned prayer. A listening ear. A studious nod. A humorous joke. Because these expressions of care build up people, they attract them back for more.

In the movie *Mary Poppins*, Mary, Burt, and the two children are in an emergency situation. Uncle Albert has become severely ill from a bout of "laughitis." The group is called in to settle him down. But instead of relieving the illness, they are overcome by the same infectious disease. Soon they too are rolling with laughter. Emotions are contagious. They take over "so quick you can't control it and so subtly that you are not really aware it is going on," says Elaine Hatfield, a psychologist at the University of Hawaii, after studying hundreds of people's reactions to emotional situations.[12] How does architecture encourage positive emotions? What makes a family atmosphere?

Gathering seating. To encourage love, people must be "on line," with visual connections between people. This is not possible in straight rows where the backs of people's heads is the only view. Thus most new churches are designed with wrap-around seating. And several older structures are remodeling to provide gathered seating, such as St. Thomas More Church, Braintree, Massachusetts; Calbury Baptist Church, Montevideo, Minnesota; and the Chapel of Mount Saint Dominic, Caldwell, New Jersey.

Cheerful setting, which includes:

*Natural light—a cleansing agent for a religion that believes "God is light and in him there is no darkness at all" (1 John 1:5).

*Padded seats—to pamper a sensitive human element.

*Brightness—thirty-five dimmable foot-candles should be the minimum via direct and/or indirect lighting. (Direct light can create glare and dark shadows on people's faces.)

*Proper crowding—50 percent to 85 percent of capacity; anything less is deadly, and anything more is sardine-like.

*Adequate spacing—three feet for chair or pew rows minimum; baby boomers are taller and bigger than their parents.

Variety: A Place That Is Creative

Variation is the spice of life, particularly to the baby boomer. It adds zest to a worship service meal and staves off boredom. What has changed in your service lately? The order, style of music, printing of bulletin, dress of pastor, or decorations? Some will object to this. "Churches have split over these issues," they will say.

I say, "There are more churches that have died from monotony than have split from variety."

This issue is so important that Roger Patterson, national architect for The United Methodist Church, calls facility flexibility the number-one priority of all church structures. And he says worship space flexibility is the number-one A priority.

Platform flexibility. Multifunctional worship is promoted by platform moldability. Let it be like a child's sandbox—big, flat, and pliable, to evolve as your styles change. First Baptist, Randolf, Maryland, remodeled its chancel for this reason. The platform was made one level and enlarged forward, the modesty rail was removed, and center stairs were added to facilitate different productions, choir sizes, weddings, and other services. Lighting and microphone locations also were designed for flexibility.

Floor plan flexibility. Many churches, like the Light of the World Catholic Church, Littleton, Colorado, promote creativity through a changeable seating plan. Shuffling the platform and seating creates a different emphasis and style for each season, a doughnut shape for Easter, corner focus for summer, against the long wall for Christmas. This may be accomplished by using movable, four-foot by four-foot stackable platform sections and hundreds of padded chairs.

Changeable colors. Have you ever tried chewing the same piece of gum for several hours? It tends to lose its flavor and become stale after about thirty minutes. But if you insert a new piece of a different flavor, your mouth is quickly tantalized again. Celebration centers with new coloration every few months can add much enjoyment to worship. Ten percent of the wall surfaces in changeable banners, decorations, plants, and drama scenery is the minimum needed to prevent worship from growing stale.

Think about times when you have felt close to God. An uplifting holiday season. The long, lonely road of a crisis. The quiet of a mountain meadow. The comfort of a daily prayer

Flexible seating promotes creativity at the Light of the World Catholic Church in Littleton, Colorado.

time. Circumstances draw us closer to the Almighty. A cozy candlelight Christmas eve service. An outdoor sunrise service on Easter, when the dawn breaks the cold darkness, and the sun dances on the dewy morning grass. The comfortable chair in a quiet den used for daily personal devotions. The breathtaking Rocky Mountain view over golden fall-covered aspen trees. All of these situations inspire us. Yes, people are "surrounding sensitive." The celebration center in a church is not everything, but it is among the most important things. As caretakers of God's celebration center, we are responsible for creating settings that help inspire others to move toward God, so God can move toward them.

VIII
INCORPORATION ROOMS

Driving through North Platte, Nebraska, during cold, crisp mornings gives you a glimpse of one of God's great designs. Along Interstate 80, several duck ponds are close to the Platte River and the road. Hundreds of resting ducks and geese fill these ponds, pausing there while making their long trek to warmer climates. As groups take off and land you begin to understand their group dynamics.

They congregate together because there is safety in numbers. There is also mutual support. By flying in the familiar "V" shape, the leader slices the wind for the others. Occasionally you will see stray ducks fly into the group, be accepted, and join the pack.

Churches are major duck ponds. As family groups fly in and out, they find an oasis—a place for refreshment, rejuvenation, and friendship.

A large celebration service does not meet all of these needs. Trying to develop friendships in a worship service would be like talking to someone who is also talking to someone else on the telephone. People cannot concentrate on two different conversations at the same time. Therefore, any church larger than sixty requires multiple small groups. Groups of ten to thirty persons can develop true lasting relationships—relationships that incorporate the support, intimacy, enjoyment, and accountability that form the foundation for long-lasting Christian growth.

Research by Flavil R. Yeakley, Jr., indicates that growing and non-growing churches have about the same number of "converts," but declining churches have a higher drop-out rate. Growing churches retain people through incorporation into small groups. Particularly important for adults are group sizes ranging from thirty to sixty.[13]

Win Arn, in *The Church Growth Ratio Book*, states: "Every new member should have a minimum of seven new friends in the church within the first six months." The implication: Inactive membership is caused by a lack of opportunity to meet others. Opportunity is provided when a church has "at least seven groups for every 100 members." And "one of every five groups [was] started in the past two years."[14]

Herb Miller describes the "sweet-sixteen principle" for congregational involvement. If the total active membership, divided by the total number of active groups, is larger than sixteen, then a church "is short on fellowship and participation opportunities."[15] If this is true, then new groups need to be formed.

Robert Bast, Elmer Towns, Leith Anderson, and Robert Schuller—all leaders in church development—recommend small groups to attract new members and nurture the existing congregation.

The celebration center is essential, but trying to build a church on that element alone is like trying to build an effective public school system by constructing only an auditorium.

Incorporation Rooms Provide a
Magnetic Pull to the Unchurched

A magnet is "(a) A body that attracts iron and certain other materials by virtue of a surrounding field of force. (b) A person, place, object, or situation that exerts attraction."[16] Small groups often are the magnets that pull in baby boomers. Many young adults are reluctant to attend a church, yet they are interested in spiritual issues. They are afraid that going to church will be like shopping for a new car. They fear that the minute they set foot in a church they will be asked for money and that the church is only interested in selling something. Small groups allow the unchurched to feel that they have circumvented the salesroom with all the flashy lights. They are attracted to the real church—the people— and they experience that in small groups.

Here are some ways churches are using their facilities to incorporate small group magnets:

Seeker events to learn about Christianity. These are seminars or workshops that investigate basic biblical truths. These small classes usually occupy an adult classroom on Sunday morning.

Issue events to give direct small-group support. New Hope Community Church in Portland, Oregon, offers "side-door" evangelism. They use small groups that meet needs—such as drug and alcohol rehabilitation, blended families, separation survival, and survivors of rape—to begin the contact and pull people in. Comfortable group-counseling rooms house these ministries effectively.

Social activities are the most common ways to do small-group evangelism. They are based on the two magnets of food and fun. Mission Hills Baptist Church, in Littleton, Colorado, mixes celebrating the Christmas season with a well-known guest speaker and a delicious meal to attract 400 women to a banquet. They also have an alternative Halloween festival that attracts 1,000 family members (one-half of whom are non-attenders) to a festive party. The unchurched see that Mission Hills is more than a bunch of stuffed boring people. They are fun-loving, family people.

Use recreation. Basketball, volleyball, and softball are the big leagues of sports evangelism. Many churches have built gymnasiums and outdoor fields for this purpose. Fellowship Community Church in Aurora, Colorado, is even constructing a rock climbing wall for its youth ministry. Competition and camaraderie are important to many. They often lead to a conversion.

Community services are the safety net for our nation's distressed. The affluence of the 1960s has crumbled into a much smaller pile. More and more of our neighbors are becoming less fortunate. This may be a temporary slide, but I believe every baby boomer will need some emotional or financial assistance sometime in his or her life. Churches are commanded to be the safety net for them (Luke 12:33), and the early church is our example (Acts 4:32-36). Community service includes food and clothing banks and shelters for the homeless. But it also may include child care for two-working-parent families or housing for the elderly.

Clifford Community Church in Gilford, New Hampshire, has turned the church building into a community center. They recently remodeled to add after-school supervision, recreation rooms for aerobics and other activities, youth rooms for Scouting, and day-care facilities. The key to their success, and that of any facility that houses small groups, is quality. To compete with the secular world, meeting rooms should look like hotel conference rooms with modern finishes, bright lighting, carpeted floors, and a table full of refreshments. Dining facilities must have quality meals, professional sound systems for speakers, real pottery plates with metal tableware, and tablecloths—similar to hotel banquet facilities. Recreation centers need full-size playing surfaces, adequate lighting, and a place to change clothes. Child care requires trained staff and professional facilities. (Contact your state department of social services for their regulations.)

One pastor says, "There are many good things to do; our job is to discern and do the best for God." Provide the best possible facilities for the magnetic small groups God wants you to organize.

Incorporation Rooms Stimulate Growth

Recently home fitness equipment sales have skyrocketed. Private health clubs are proliferating. And church work-out rooms are also multiplying. Most church addition and remodeling projects under construction today include exercise areas. These places fulfill the command: "Work out your own salvation" (Phil. 2:12). They are places where small groups exercise their spiritual gifts as servants of God's people. They are places where newcomers get plugged in, where old-timers share their wisdom, and where children have fun learning the basics of our faith, and baby boomers fulfill their desire to:

better themselves through the knowledge and wisdom of others;
be challenged and held accountable;
invest their lives in helping others;
discuss today's issues and determine how the Bible is their guide.

Many churches have their exercise group meet outside the facilities. They may use home locations for Bible studies, "TLC" groups, house churches, and fellowship events. But most churches utilize a Sunday morning small-group format. Often called Sunday school, it usually has higher attendance rates than do small groups that meet in outside facilities. Some churches have up to 90 percent of their worship attenders in Sunday school. But few churches attract more than 75 percent in class sizes ranging from twenty to sixty.

A healthy small-group program develops classes for all ages. The groups are usually divided by age and life situation—that is, fourth- and fifth-grade boys or girls; post-college singles; or pre-retirement, children-living-at-home couples. The key is offering a variety of different opportunities so people can comfortably choose a group they enjoy and relate to.

The goal of each group is to facilitate spiritual strengthening. If this is done, the groups will grow numerically and should be divided regularly. The starting of new groups is a major growth factor for any church. Five-year-old groups tend to have friendships firmly established. New groups are where most new people feel comfortable. Thus, as Win Arn recommends, one in five groups should be less than two years old.

According to *The Church Planter*[17] the following is a balanced age breakdown and space allocation for Sunday schools. The numbers represent balanced percentages of Sunday school attendance in healthy churches:

Nursery:	0-2 yr. old	8%	25-30	S.F./person
Beginner:	3-4 yr. old	6%	25	S.F./person
Primary:	Kind.-2nd gr.	10%	20	S.F./person
Junior:	3rd-6th gr.	10%	18	S.F./person
Jr. High:	7th-9th gr.	16%	16	S.F./person
Sr. High:	10th-12th gr.	10%	14	S.F./person
Adults:	post high sch.	50%	12	S.F./person

These numbers are very similar to the recommended space breakdowns of the Southern Baptist Convention, the Church of the Nazarene, and The United Methodist Church.

These space allocations are advisable guidelines. There are many variables, including room efficiency, type of programming, style of furniture and arrangement, storage, size of classes, and so on that could require more or less space. Double-check each classroom's capacity against present and projected enrollment. Classes that exceed capacity can be relocated according to the following criteria:

Nursery: See chapter 6.

Beginner, primary, and junior: Close to lobby, especially for younger ages. Group locations that progress down a hall by grade levels are much easier for newcomers to find. Scattered locations confuse everyone. Several churches use large rooms with movable dividers for sound and visual buffering. This allows for multipurpose rooms to double as dining, recreational, and classrooms.

Junior and senior highs desire places that are secluded and create a separate identity. Let the youth redecorate their rooms every few years and create a hang out center. Soundproofing is desired, because the youth will want to play some music, do some roughhousing, and sing.

Adults are very finicky. Carpet, comfortable seats in a circle, a dry erasable marker board, good lighting at thirty-five foot-candles, soundproofing, and a table full of coffee and refreshments are the minimums. They often desire air conditioning, natural light, and modern finishes.

Some churches, like Calvary Community Baptist Church in Northglenn, Colorado, are using the Master Teacher concept. They have a lecture to all adults in the auditorium, then break down into small groups for discussion. This utilizes the worship space more efficiently, and the acoustics are not a problem if there are more than three groups in a room.

Central Community Church has all the bases covered, with oodles of opportunities for incoming families. They have seventy "TLC" groups that minister throughout the week in people's homes. The groups of fifteen to twenty include a Bible study, singing, sharing, and prayer. But they also have about 75 percent of their worship attendance in fifty Sunday school classes. The program has even been recognized by the state of Kansas for its contribution to the citizens. The Center of Christian Growth is weekly training doctrine, Bible, and church history. The Family Life Counseling Center offers seminars on family issues and counseling to both the community and the congregation. In 1989, they offered a new seminar through the Sunday school. "Your Family Can Be Fun" pulled in four hundred first-time visitors to the church.

Nutritious Small Groups

Matthew 28:18-20 calls churches to their ultimate purpose: to make disciples. This challenge can be accomplished only with small groups. They are like the vegetables in a seven-course meal. They are not the main ticket, nor are they very glamorous. But they are full of essential ingredients—vitamins that develop strong, healthy, and powerful church bodies:

Vitamin A: Admonish one another (Col. 3:16)
Vitamin B1: Build up one another (1 Thess. 5:11)
Vitamin B2: Bearing one another's burdens (Gal. 6:2)
Vitamin C: Confess your sins to one another (James 5:16)
Vitamin E: Encourage one another (1 Thess. 5:11)

Vitamin F: Forgive one another (Col. 3:13)
Vitamin L: Love one another (Rom. 12:10)
Vitamin P: Pray for one another (James 5:16)

These vitamins are most effectively absorbed through small-group vegetables. Serving up these ingredients in effective church buildings is a key to transmitting them. The flavor and aroma will incorporate hundreds of people into your church.

IX

DISABLED DELIVERED

Jerusalem newspaper headlines from about A.D. 33 might have read:

Paralytic healed by Jesus of Nazareth
Another paralytic given legs by Nazarene
Jesus healed hemorrhage and "dead" daughter on Thursday
Two blind men believe, given sight
Speechless man has much to say, "Thanks, Jesus"

Clearly, Jesus had—and still has—compassion for the handicapped. But many of today's "hospital orderlies" have bolted the door. "Only the healthy can see Jesus," they say. Only those who can walk, see, and hear are privileged enough to enter most churches. The forty-three million Americans with disabilities are often shut out, walled off, or segregated. And what about the millions of temporarily hampered Americans? It's difficult enough for them to deal with their twisted ankles or broken legs without feeling "locked out" of church. They want and need to celebrate along with the rest of us.

In 1990, Congress passed a law to make most public

buildings accessible to everyone. After January 1, 1992, most public entities must respond to the Americans with Disabilities Act (ADA). As of 1992, the exceptions to the ADA are religious organizations and private clubs, which are exempt, But there are exceptions to the exceptions: If a church has ever or will ever lease space to a non-religious organization, and the use is considered a public accommodation, then the ADA applies to the areas used by the outside organization. An example is a local community group or a private, independent day-care center. Many churches lease space for Boy Scouts, local concerts, conference seminars, and the like. If a church will be used by these types of groups, then its structures are subject to the law. If a church plans to remain isolated, it should still strongly consider the ADA as a ministry guideline.

The following is an explanation of how the ADA affects church structures.

Readily Achievable Existing Structures

This is the definition of the work immediately required on existing structures. They are minor building adjustments that remove handicap barriers without much difficulty or expense. Generally, they will not require structural changes. They are also not required if they impose an undue financial hardship on the owner of a building. Regardless of the law, every church should make every effort to conform to these modest measures:

1. Installing bathroom grab bars.
2. Ramping stepped access points—front stoops, short interior stairs, outdoor curbs, etc.
3. Protect or remove protruding objects from hallways that may harm people who are blind, including objects that start more than twenty-seven inches above the floor and protrude more than four inches—coat racks, bookshelves, countertops, artwork, and so on. If objects cannot be removed, then construct a protective wall railing or base to warn people of the hazard.

4. Reduce door thresholds that are higher than one-half inch. Anything taller is a mountain for wheelchairs to traverse.

5. Eliminate the need to grab and turn round doorknobs. Install one of the following (contact a local hardware store for manufacturers):
   (a) new locks with lever handles;
   (b) universal levers added to existing round knobs;
   (c) automatic door opening hardware.

6. Change door closures to allow access before the door closes (seven-second delay). Also reduce the opening force to only five pound-feet.

7. Install stairway and ramp handrails at the correct height and length. Both sides of a stair or ramp, with one-and-one-half to two-inch diameter handrails. Position the top of the rail at thirty-four to thirty-eight inches above the floor surfaces and extend the railing over the top landing twelve inches, and twelve inches plus stair depth over the bottom landing.

8. Provide parking spaces for persons with handicapping conditions, eight feet wide with a five foot-wide access aisle on one side. The number of handicapped parking spaces shall be 4 percent, up to 125: 1 percent per 100 above 125.

9. Install toilet fixtures at proper heights. At least one handicap-access stall per public toilet room for each sex requires:
   (a) toilet with rim height of seventeen to nineteen inches above floor;
   (b) maximum urinal rim height of seventeen inches above floor;
   (c) rearranging toilet partitions around handicapped stall to increase floor size to three feet by five feet nine inches or five feet by five feet, and door swings out;
   (d) lavatory underclearance of twenty-nine inches and maximum rim height of thirty-four inches;
   (e) bottom of mirror height a maximum of forty inches above floor;

(f) insulate exposed lavatory pipes;

(g) paper cup, paper towel, and other dispensers cannot be more than forty-eight inches from floor to dispensing height;

10. Install paper cup dispensers near drinking fountains if the waterspout is more than thirty-six inches above the floor.

11. Add raised letters to elevator control buttons.

12. Rearrange tables, chairs, vending machines, and display racks to allow minimum thirty-six-inch aisle clearances.

13. Lower wall telephones and controls to forty-eight inches above floor.

14. Install flashing fire alarm lights.

15. Install offset hinges to widen doorway access to thirty-two inches minimum.

16. Eliminate turnstiles or provide alternate access route.

17. Replace high-pile, low-density carpet.

18. Remove pews or chairs to allow wheelchair locations three-feet wide and four-feet deep minimum, number to equal:

1 space for 4 to 25 seating capacity
2 spaces for 26 to 50
4 spaces for 51 to 300
5 spaces for 301 to 500
6+ 1 space for each 100 seats over 500.

This is a list of adjustments each church should strongly consider. A complete list can be obtained from a local building official or The Christian League for the Handicapped, Box 948, Walworth, WI 53184, 414-275-6131, or by calling the Architectural and Transportation Barriers Compliance Board, 800-USA-ABLE.

Alterations Like New

Now comes the complicated part—blending the new and the old parts of the building. At times, this can seem almost as challenging as trying to mix two different thousand-piece jigsaw puzzles of the United States. The pieces will not mesh without some careful planning and reshaping. You will have difficulty adjusting any building addition or renovation to the existing structure. Adding handicapped accessibility to this merger often makes the compromises required even more painful.

The Americans with Disabilities Act requires that all alterations to a building be like new. This means that in any renovation, remodeling, and additions the handicap accessibility rules apply to everything that affects the use of both the old and the new parts of a building.

The following examples illustrate how the ADA rules apply to church alterations.

*A two-story church structure offers weekly meals to the elderly through an outside organization. But to be more effective they want to expand their dining and kitchen facilities on the basement level. The new dining and kitchen facilities will require handicap accessibility. Also the way people travel from outside the building to the eating area will need accessibility via a ramp or elevator. Telephones, drinking fountains, and restrooms will need to accommodate use for all as well. In short, the accessibility standards also apply to the areas being modified, the "path of travel," and any required auxiliary uses.

*If a church wants to add a gymnasium and will allow outside groups to use it, then the gym, restrooms, and route to the area must be handicap accessible.

*If a church intends to have community concerts in its sanctuary, it will need to remodel the platform route, seating, and toilets.

The exception to these "alternatives like new" requirements are listed below:

1. A church building that is and will be used only by in-house church groups—no Scouts, preschool, etc.—is exempt from ADA rules.

2. Normal maintenance—such as reroofing, mechanical modifications, carpeting, or painting—that does not change how a room is used is exempt from ADA rules.

3. Fully applying the handicap accessibility requirements is not always possible, such as when widening a hallway that has bearing walls on both sides cannot be done without tearing down the building and starting over. In this case the new construction "shall provide the maximum physical accessibility feasible."[18]

4. Structures that are "eligible for listing in the National Register of Historic Places, or are designated historic under state or local law"[19] are required to be handicapp accessible, but only to the extent that this does not destroy the historical significance of the building. This judgment process will be determined by the State Historic Preservation Officer or Advisory Council of Historic Preservation. (There is also a list of alternative regulations that may be used when remodeling a historic structure.)

5. An elevator does not need to be installed for buildings that are less than three stories, or less than 3,000 square feet per floor. An exception to this exception is offices used for mental health care. If a church facility will let an outside counseling group use a second-story office that has been remodeled, then an elevator must be provided.

6. An owner must spend only an additional 20 percent on the access route and auxiliary uses. Anything more is considered an undue hardship and excessive. If the cost to fully comply with the rules is excessive, then the monies may be spent in the following order:

An accessible entrance.
An accessible route to the remodeled or added area.
At least one handicap-access unisex toilet.
Accessible telephone(s).
Accessible drinking fountain(s).
Accessible parking, storage, fire alarms.

The law becomes complex when a church adds on to its facilities but does not intend to allow an outside group to use them. This opens the possibility for future litigation. What happens if twenty years later a new pastor and church board change their minds and rent the facility to a group? If a person with a handicapping condition wants to join the group but cannot because of nonconforming facilities, then the church is open to legal action.

Every building alteration must be carefully thought through, for the nineties and beyond. Consider the legal implications, but also the ministry effects. Does God want you to minister to disabled persons? One in six Americans has a permanent disability, and thousands of others are temporarily hampered. Is your church making Christianity into an exclusive club reserved only for the privileged?

Joni Erickson Tada has written several books on faith and dealing with life struggles that have helped countless persons. She writes poetry and is featured on several recording albums. Her paintings also are world renowned. She is a tremendous speaker and leader of a non-profit ministry. Her life has affected millions of people for Jesus Christ. Yet, she is often hampered by inadequate church facilities. Joni is a quadriplegic. Her handicap prevents her from helping people in churches that cannot invite her to speak. And these buildings and ministries are handicapped by their inability to invite people like her. Do not let a building disable the goals of your ministry.

X

ALTERATION ALTERNATIVES

The Wooddale Church Expansion Committee had to make a tough decision. Had they thoroughly examined all of the possibilities? They were at three services but were still overcrowded. A suburban Minneapolis church of 1,200 attendees, they owned less than twenty parking spaces. Their shortage of sanctuary seating and education facilities also stifled growth. What should they do? Relocate or add on?

Their initial attempts to alleviate the overcrowding included purchasing as many of the surrounding houses as possible. They thought that if they owned the block, they could raze the houses and build needed parking spaces and education facilities. But five of the seventeen homeowners would not sell. Also, the city zoning laws would not permit tearing down the houses to install a parking lot or building an addition to the church. Therefore, their only alternative was to sell and move to a new location. Looking back across the ten years, they see that their choice was painful but well worth the effort. Today, their attendance is more than three thousand each Sunday.

The Grace Church Expansion Committee also had some tough decisions. Theirs was another suburban, landlocked

Minneapolis church that had outgrown its facilities. But instead of moving, they were able to expand parking and build a 1,000-seat sanctuary. The difference? They had acquired enough land to expand. They also went to multiple services and began sending out hundreds of members to organize new churches. Today they continue to grow at their original location.

These two entirely different churches had very similar circumstances but went in opposite directions. How do you weigh these kinds of choices?

First Priority: Stewardship

The parable of the talents in Matthew 25:14-28 gives us a clear picture of what these two churches desired. With God as its master, a "good and faithful" church invests in the opportunities God gives it. Wooddale's only opportunity lay in the direction of moving. Grace's best choice was to stay put. The structural results were different, but they fulfilled the same goal: to be good stewards of the ministry God has given them; good stewards of the financial resources, and good stewards in making a place that will satisfy both the ministry objectives and the available resources. God has given these churches many talents, both figuratively and monetarily. The churches returned much more. Now God is giving them much much more.

As good stewards the leaders of these churches had to ask the right questions: (1) Are they using the present facilities in the most efficient means? (2) If the present facilities are not enough, what augmentation is needed? (3) If the present location is not enough, where should they move? They also asked the right questions in the right order, for the right reasons, while looking for the right answers.

The right order for asking these three questions starts with the presumption that *less is more:* The less a church spends on facilities, the more it can focus on ministry. Most churches have ample accommodations; they just need to become more efficient. Only after their present facilities are cramped to capacity will they need to expand. And only after their present property is cramped to capacity will they need to relocate.

The right reason for asking these three questions impregnates facility design like water fills the ocean. Water is the ocean; likewise, a godly and pure church is required to fill a church structure. An edifice mentality can cripple a church just as badly as gossip and envy can. Proper facilities are a way of achieving a proper ministry; they are not the goal.

Why, then, do so many churches ask the right questions, in the right order, and for the right reason, but end up with the wrong answers? Sometimes, the leaders have predetermined the answers. In other instances, they have limited the answers they are willing to hear because of stifling local or denominational traditions. In either case, a church ends up a poor steward. Although it is among the most difficult challenges they can understand, as a matter of integrity a church's leaders must continually examine the motives behind the answers they are willing to hear or not hear.

Efficient Church Edifices

To some people, striving for an "efficient" church edifice is a senseless goal. "Churches are for worshiping God," they say, "not for achieving an efficiency rating." Yes, church facilities are for worship. But they are also for education, fellowship, recreation, counseling, and Bible study. As churches expand their uses by serving a growing number of diverse groups, they must become much more efficient today than ever before.

The best way to begin maximizing building use is to ask these three questions: (1) When and where is the peak use? (2) Is it in the celebration center on Sunday morning? (3) If so, can the peak use be divided into two or three services?

These are the best beginning questions because the easiest, and by far the least expensive, way to accommodate tight facilities is with a double or triple schedule on Sunday morning. For many small churches, there may be a problem of staffing the extra programs. But expending the energy to work through these objectives is by far easier than the other two alternatives—building expansion or living with your conscience as your cramped building stifles numerical growth.

Multiple services have other advantages, as well.

Different worship styles can be developed in alternative time periods. Many people enjoy an informal, contemporary early service. Herb Miller, in his book *The Vital Congregation,* predicts that adding a second service usually increases the total worship attendance by 5 to 15 percent. The more the styles of the two services differ to satisfy two segments of the congregation, the greater the attendance growth.[20] For example, go for traditional versus contemporary, formal versus casual, and intimate versus impersonal.

Some people prefer a different time for worship—to either sleep in or get chores done before service. Others prefer to go to early service so they can have the bulk of the day left for recreation. Also, many American workers do *not* work traditional nine to five, Monday to Friday jobs. They have weekend careers that require them to miss traditional service times. A Saturday evening service allows them to attend. Many Catholic churches have offered Saturday evening masses for years. More and more Protestants are moving in this direction.

After you have looked at your celebration center use, the second logical set of questions would focus on the other parts of the building. Is every room used to maximum efficiency? Can room use be reshuffled to achieve greater volume of ministry per week? With a floor plan of the building, examine how each room is used. Determine:

1. The area of each room;
2. The use of each room;
3. The required area per person for the use (see chapter 8, nursery at thirty square feet per child);
4. The design capacity of each room (the area of each room divided by the required area per person);
5. The comfort capacity (85 percent of the design capacity, or multiply the design capacity by 0.85);

6. Compare the comfort capacity of each room with the present attendance (if the comfort capacity is larger than the attendance, the room can be used by more people; if the comfort capacity is smaller than the attendance, the class would work better if it relocated or divided);
7. Compare the comfort capacity with the projected attendance five years from now.

This room-by-room review probably indicates that some rooms are overburdened, some will soon be overburdened, and some are underutilized. In this process, ask whether some classes can be relocated to a room that better fits their class size. Sometimes a large class in a small room can decide to start a new class (which usually involves more total attendees). Two smaller classes can sometimes be combined into a larger space with a temporary wall or movable divider.

Is furniture cramping space? Can furniture be replaced or rearranged to accommodate more people? Ray Bowman suggests in "How to Maximize Your Current Space" that churches can increase worship capacity by switching from pews to chairs.[21] Movable chairs also allow for multiple use. Other furniture ideas to consider:

*Removing tables in classrooms saves 30 percent space.
*Instead of seating class members in a large circle, place them in rows forming a "U" or in rows that face each other. This encourages eye contact, while allowing larger numbers of persons in the same amount of space.
*Utilizing child-size furniture creates a better learning environment and adds space to rooms for younger ages.
*Two-tiered nursery cribs take up much less space and are designed for greater safety.
*Moving classrooms outside in warm climates frees up valuable inside space.
*Banquet seating is greater at rectangular tables than at round ones.
*Removing foyer furniture from cramped quarters is sometimes important in creating a loving atmosphere.

*Platform furniture may overcrowd and clutter a worship service. In some instances, the pastor and worship assistants can conveniently sit in the front row (which is usually empty anyway). Many churches are reducing the bulk of platform furniture to create the more informal atmosphere that many baby boomers desire. This includes pulpits, lecterns, communion tables, railings, and chairs.

Is there valuable underutilized space available anywhere in the building? If so, are minor adjustments required to make it usable? Many nooks and crannies are like pearls waiting to be found in underwater clams. Unused and somewhat rough, they can be polished through the application of imagination. These unused areas are usually behind the platform, near the rear seating of a sanctuary, in the attic, or in the basement.

Some of these "out of the way" areas are perfect for older children's classrooms. Third graders and older youth enjoy the separation. They also like the idea of going through the catacombs to get to a place like that. These spaces can also be used for youth or music rooms. These areas may need some additional lighting, a new coat of paint, carpeting, and new heating. But these are minor issues compared to the cost of adding onto a church. Just be sure there is adequate exiting in case of an emergency.

Thousands of older church structures have extra nave seating but lack adequate classroom or lobby space. With five-year projections, most of them could remove several rows of seating to help meet other ministry needs. If done properly, the space can serve a dual role. Faith Community Church in Littleton, Colorado, has a glass wall with large doors that separate its loving lobby from the celebration center. Calvary Evangelical Free Church, Broomfield, Colorado, has movable partitions that separate six classrooms from the sanctuary. Both options allow for overflow seating.

Can multi-use space increase special ministry success? Unquestionably! The single-use room is becoming as obsolete as the phonograph. Churches cannot afford the

Movable partitions at the back of the sanctuary can be closed for classroom space or opened to expand sanctuary seating.

luxury of letting expensive single-use spaces sit idle. A few new structures are designed so carefully that a single room may be used in six different ways: for worship, as a classroom, for dining, for recreation, for a children's club, and as a youth room.

For an existing room(s), a few adjustments will easily double or triple use. The options that give the greatest opportunities are:

1. *Tacoize ingredients.* Combine several classrooms into a larger recreation and/or banquet facility. Or divide a large recreation/banquet room into smaller classrooms. This, the most common multi-use adaptation, usually involves movable walls that can be opened to create large spaces or closed to produce numerous private smaller classrooms. Churches like St. Paul's Lutheran, Denver, Colorado, and First Baptist in Grand Island, Nebraska, have created these rooms.

Fireside room off lobby is multi-purpose—classroom, chapel, or expanded lobby.

Replacing fixed walls with movable partitions between a narthex and adjacent classrooms can double or triple the narthex area. Columbine Hills in Littleton, Colorado, designed this into their new facilities. The classroom space also doubles as a fireside room for small socials. With overstuffed furniture, a huge rock fireplace, and soft lighting, the environment is very comfortable and cozy for many different kinds of gatherings.

2. *Uncuff sanctuaries.* Remove restrictive fixed pews and platforms from a sanctuary to create a sanctuary/fellowship hall/recreational combination. The purist will object to desecrating a worship area. But the pragmatists—which many boomers are—will endorse the triple function. Care must be taken, of course, to preserve the appropriate environment for each—a religious worship area, a comfortable eating space, and toughness for recreation. The multiple tasks require careful planning of the floor covering, lighting,

acoustics, and protection of equipment, windows, and other furnishings. Also, each use may require support facilities (such as kitchen, storage, or sound equipment). If Billy Graham can change Yankee Stadium into a worship environment, can we not change a worship environment into a recreation area and back? Or how about the Iowa cornfield transformed into a place to conduct sacred Mass for Pope John Paul II?

In the 1960s a new invention swept across America. It sliced, sawed, screwed, and served its way into American camping hearts. The Swiss Army knife transformed a single-use pocket knife into a masterful tool for every backwoods experience. It became so popular that it was the basis for a television show. In the late 1980s, MacGyver combined the multifunctional instrument with his intellect and ingenuity to capture television viewers' hearts. In churches that require more space for more uses, multi-use rooms are stealing the hearts of many property committees. They fulfill the functional requirements without the cost of building additions.

Can any of the rooms be located elsewhere—out of the building, or even completely off the church property? Yes, placing all of a church's tools in one box is more convenient. People are more enthusiastic about a ministry if they can see where it is located. But sometimes a church cannot stuff all the utensils into one container. This is when choices have to be made: What instruments are used most often? Which functions will work just as well in other localities? A carpenter's work belt may contain a necessary hammer, nails, chalkline, screw gun, tape measure, pencil, and square. It usually does not carry a saw or crowbar because they are too bulky. Which rooms in your building fit each of these descriptions?

Storage is the number-one way space is wasted. It steals area and swipes finances (because area is money). Give the boot to every item that is not used monthly—the Christmas props, spring decorations, scenery for musicals, materials used during fund drives, and the 1960s accounting records. Move them all out to a storage shed or to a rented self-storage garage. In that process you also may see some ridiculous possessions you have been "pack ratting" and dispose of them. For the essential items, renting a garage is less expensive than adding classroom space.

What group gatherings can meet off campus, thereby relieving space stress? Some adult classes can meet in homes, schools, or community centers. Youth groups can sometimes rent a senior high school gymnasium. Churches adjacent to office buildings often rent office space for classrooms. Vineyard Church in Wheatridge, Colorado, uses an adjacent shopping center to house children's classrooms. Casper United Methodist Church in Casper, Wyoming, uses a restaurant for fellowship dinners and banquets. The key: be creative and flexible.

Sometimes, church offices can be moved off campus. A close location is always important, but an adjacent office building or commercial space can often be converted quickly. Christ Community, East Metro Community, and South Evangelical Presbyterian are all Denver churches with offices located off campus. Mission Hills Baptist Church, Littleton, Colorado, located its counseling center off campus to better serve the public.

The secret to efficiency in church structures is to continuously remind ourselves that the building is not the church. It is only a tool. There is nothing sacred about its materials. For some people, memorials have become sacred. A pew, room, or artwork may become idols that hinder rearrangement. Perhaps the founding pastor has been honored with a chapel dedicated to his name, or a wealthy businessperson paid for an addition. These memorials can take on the life of a ghost defending the territory for all eternity. But educated, motivated church leaders can work through those issues to provide efficient structures.

Augmentation Versus Navigation

If present facilities are not enough, then what? The two choices are augmentation and navigation. Augmentation means enlarging your structure by adding on the spaces necessary. Navigation means finding a new or additional location. How does a church know what is best?

Leaders should strongly consider augmentation when the following factors point toward remaining at the present site:

Visibility is high. The greater the number of people who know your location, the greater your potential to serve them.

Access is convenient. Churches have grown in potential influence from neighborhood to regional institutions. The more people who can arrive at your church within a fifteen- to twenty-minute drive time, the more there are who will come. Location near, and access from, major thoroughfares is a must.

Acreage is available and affordable—either already owned or potentially owned. A rule of thumb: One acre of land supports about 100 to 125 worshipers and an additional 75 in classrooms at any one time. This is a very general guideline and depends greatly on zoning laws, buildability of land, and type of ministry. It also assumes a two-story church structure and standard parking layout. Project your ministry size at least five to ten years into the future. Then divide by an adjusted capacity to determine acreage availability.

Buildability. Is the property usable? Consider such issues as zoning, utility access, land features, soil conditions, adjacent neighbors, and high water tables.

Ministry focus. Does your ministry center on the people in the region? Are you a traditional church in the midst of non-traditional neighbors? Does your congregation commute to worship? To whom does God want you to minister? Locate your church structure where your ministry is.

Healthy architecture. A wholesome structure has simple, clean circulation patterns, a logical layout of rooms, and the ability to be added onto. An unhealthy structure has been added onto in disjointed pieces. People get confused when they try to locate rooms in a labyrinth of hallways. Adding to this kind of structure will only add to the junk.

Increased salability. To a church whose feet are cemented into the ground, this principle is not useful. But churches who are certain they will relocate sometime should consider their ability to sell. Smaller, newer churches comprise most of the church hunting market. Their funds and their needs demand a smaller structure. Therefore, a church may not be increasing its building's salability by adding on.

Unbearable burden. Finances always play a key role in decision making. Since augmentation is usually less expensive than relocation and building from scratch, it is usually the best economic choice. But do not always think it is the wisest choice. Sometimes adding on is like throwing good money after bad (see "Healthy architecture," above).

Mind-set. Some churches are firmly entrenched, and to rip them from their location would be a declaration of war. Other congregations are open to all the possibilities, including relocation. If your congregation is filled with the former, then focus only on facility augmentation.

Every church must consider each of the areas listed above before deciding what to do with its facilities. There is no right answer, except what is best for your circumstances, but negative response in any one of these areas probably forces a navigation. Take your time. Pray through every issue on every location you are considering. Wisdom is not instantaneous. It usually takes about one to three years to find the right answers (see James 1:5).

For Second Baptist Church in Houston, the wisdom pointed toward augmentation. In the mid 1980s they purchased land to add a 6,200-seat sanctuary at a staggering cost of $51 million for land and structure. Today, the choice seems to have been wise.

In 1983, Central Community in Wichita, Kansas, decided moving was God's answer. Their land-locked location would have required $1.5 million to acquire a few inner-city lots. A large suburban property would be equal in cost and have twice the visibility, access, and usability. Their move was time-consuming, but worth the effort.

The Church on the Way, Van Nuys, California, decided that both staying and moving were appropriate. Instead of fighting adding on or relocation, they purchased a second campus within one-fourth of a mile of the first. The transaction added a 2,400-seat auditorium and 125,000 square feet to Church on the Way's room inventory.

Mesa Verde Mystery

For archaeologists, Mesa Verde in southwestern Colorado remains one of the great mysteries of prehistoric times. In the thirteenth century the Anasazi Indians built their magnificent cliff dwellings there. As the years passed, they added on and remodeled until many of these dwellings resembled a modern resort condominium project rather than an ancient village. Some of the structures rose fifty feet high. We do not know why the Anasazi ended their use of the cliff dwellings. Did they abandon them because they could not be expanded for the growing tribe? Maybe the Anasazi realized that the poor access was hampering crop development. Or maybe the salability was perfect for another tribe, and the original tribe needed another place. Whatever the reason, they were wrestling with the same issues that many modern-day churches face: remodeling, adding on, relocation—alteration alternatives.

Most church leaders would prefer to avoid the complex decisions; they create so many possibilities for conflict and mistake-making. But there is something far more dangerous than discussing alteration alternatives—pretending that not discussing them is a sensible alternative, and thereby limiting your church's ministry abilities.

XI

ORGANIZING FOR THE OPERATION

You cannot decide whether you should see your doctor. The pain in your lower right abdomen may be indigestion, but it is becoming intense. Finally you decide to see your physician. She takes one look and says it is appendicitis, an inflammation of the vermiform appendix. If not removed in a matter of minutes, it will rupture, causing infection and maybe death. She orders an ambulance to take you to the hospital for an emergency operation. How do you respond? Do you brush off this advice by saying you want to consider the ramifications for a year or two? After all, you are busy at work, the kitchen remodeling needs to be finished, and your third child needs braces. Besides, you are a healthy thirtysomething, and God will take care of you.

You will probably decide to agree with the doctor, your reason being that if you do not immediately take care of your health, the important issues like work, family, and God will be immaterial because you will be dead. So you are whisked to the operating room. Once there, the hospital staff consisting of a head nurse, a scrub nurse, a surgeon, an anesthesiologist, and an assistant are fully prepared for the procedure. They have studied the order of action, know the responsibilities, and have the equipment prepared.

Churches often find themselves in a similar position. Yes, the ministry activities in which they are engaged are more important than the building. But sometimes the facilities can be a royal pain. As a pastor or church leader, you may recognize the problem. The crumbling building will not go away. It will only get worse. You need a building doctor, but helping a large group of people come to a decision is much more complex than deciding to have an appendectomy. What do you do? How do you prepare the congregation for action?

Definition of the Vision

Vision is the inspirational prelude to all human accomplishments. A world-class sprinter focuses on the finish line. A cabinetmaker has drawings of the finished product. Moses had the burning bush. Paul found his sense of direction by meeting Christ on the road.

Vision is the genesis of all God's victories. A vision is more than a vague dream; it is a recipe for action. The following is a list of ways to create a successful building vision. Their specific application will be determined by your situation. But each ingredient is essential to helping a group move from analysis to action.

1. Define your community of influence. Most people base church choices on life-style and needs. How do people in your community live? Demographic information can give you the life-style description. Sex, median-age, typical marital status, and educational levels are all areas that define the type of community you minister in. But do not overlook the emotional issues: love, acceptance, and support system also define community life-style. Try to understand both the intellectual and the emotional needs, then design your church's ministries to fulfill them.

If you do not know the demographics of your community, ask. Survey your congregation and neighborhoods. Why do people go to church or not go to church? How could your church better serve them? This is how the famous Willow Creek Community Church, northwest of Chicago, started its ministry. A simple community survey and a listening heart were keys to their beginning and continued strength.

2. Define the purpose of your church. With the information above, develop strategies for the needed ministries. Eliminate worn-out "toys" that are favorite ideas from decades past but no longer work. Fix the broken but necessary programs. Invent new ministries for new issues. Avoid saying, "We never did it that way before." Imagine what God wants you to do in five or ten years. Develop a vision.

The dreams that are the most sharply defined are the most likely to succeed. Therefore, take time to develop overall themes and goals that are specific, measurable, and achievable. Write these down and keep track of them to see whether they were attained in the expected time frame or need adjusting.

3. Define the spatial requirements. What is the ideal setting for the ministry defined above? How many people will you serve? What type of lighting, room finishes and colors, room shapes and locations, toilet locations, and storage will you need? Expand on this list. Define the optional support facilities for the various ministries. (They were listed in the previous chapters, but you will have to adapt these ideas to your situation.) Write all the ideas down first, then prioritize them according to importance and available funding.

4. Define your present building. How close do our ideals duplicate reality? Can you reshuffle the puzzle pieces to fit better? What pieces could be easily replaced to attain a better fit? How important are the missing pieces? Decide among the alternatives of remodeling, addition, or relocation.

5. Define the professionals. Many churches are reluctant to consult an architect. "The cost is prohibitive," they say. But the cost of not hiring a qualified architect is often paid in something other than money. Often, that bill is paid in people the church could have served but lost the opportunity to serve. A poorly designed building may save money, but in achieving quantity without quality it may spend much of its future ministry potentials.

Contact denominational leaders or your local chapter of the American Institute of Architects. They can probably pass along several names of architects who specialize in church design. Summarize your situation and ask these architects for a statement of qualifications. Have them include a list of past church projects (size, location, contact person, cost, photographs), a company brochure, and the resumes of key personnel. Narrow the list to three names and interview these architects and visit several of their projects. A team relationship is essential between a church and an architect. Factors like personality, communication, credentials, and ability to design a structure for your situation should have the major influence on your final selection decisions, not fees alone.

6. Define funding. Every church project requires balanced funding. It is like a three-legged stool—cut off one or two legs and the project teeters. Obviously, each church situation is different. Because the ground under the stool is not level, you will have to customize the length of each leg to fit your ministry. But 95 percent of all church projects require all three areas of financing in some form.

Leg One: Cold, hard cash. Usually about 25 percent of the total cost of a project (building, land, construction costs, utility fees, furniture, architectural/engineering fees) is paid for with hard currency. Most of the up-front costs require liquid assets, including all the fees and a down payment on land.

Leg Two: Proven pledges. Fund-raising campaigns usually try to raise a maximum of two to two-and-one-half times a church's annual budget in three-year pledges. These pledges need to be sufficient to cover about 25 percent of the total costs. Professional fund raisers have proven methods and usually raise a far higher amount than can any type of home-grown program. Obtain a list of potential fund raisers through your denomination or from other churches. Fund raisers need to be chosen the same way you would choose other professionals. Check their references, past experience, and methods. The closer these match your goals, the better.

Leg Three: Reasonable debt. Debt can be an ugly four-letter word. We all would like to see church projects constructed free and clear. Unfortunately, the vast majority of large projects require about 50 percent amortization.

Let debt bridge the vision. However, it cannot bridge the Grand Canyon; there are reasonable limits. Future ministries are at stake. Prudent rules put mortgages at:

*Not more than two to three times the annual church budget;
*Not more than one-third of the annual church budget to pay debt reduction;
*Not more than 50 percent of the total property appraisal (when the building is completed).

If these limits are exceeded, consider phasing the construction over several years. Or consider reducing the costs by adding some value engineering, a reevaluation of construction costs or methods to maintain the basic design features while eliminating some of the fancy elements. Sometimes it is better to reduce initial costs than to let the debt become a noose that hangs a ministry in a continued need to shortchange the annual operating budget for several years.

Debt can give a church access to future growth. It can be a gate of opportunity. Or it can be a loaded gun that succeeds at killing the potential of a ministry. The savings and loan debacle of the early 1990s is proof that debt decisions can exceed the limits of sound practice. Reasonable balancing, using the three criteria listed above, can protect a church's leaders from that dishonor.

Round Them Up and Move Them Out

This cry was used to drive cattle from the range to the market. Churches need to gather people together before they can be brought into an updated structure. Unity, community, and harmony are commanded under the Lordship of God (1 Cor. 1:10). We are to be in concert, even when there are different instruments—unity in the midst of diversity. To achieve a harmonious tune, all the different parts must be played properly. The group members must agree on their responsibilities. They must agree to communicate thoroughly, and pledge that when there are differences, they will seek compromise. The diagram below is a structure commonly used to achieve unity.

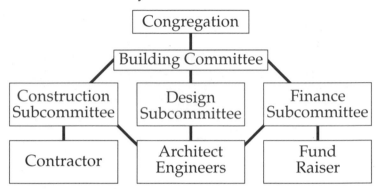

In this common structure of a building committee, some churches will combine committees or add additional tasks, such as prayer, advertising/communication, land acquisition, and so on. This usually depends on the size and organizational framework of the church and the personal expertise of key members.

The building committee is accountable to the congregation. It usually consists of a chairperson, the chairperson of each subcommittee, a few at-large members, and a pastor (sometimes the senior pastor, sometimes associates). Each subcommittee has a clearly defined role:

*Finances—to determine fund raising, debt financing (if required), memorials, payment schedule, construction budget, etc.

*Construction—to determine the type of construction contract, schedule, select contractor, and be the liaison between church and contractor during construction.

*Design—to select the architect through an interview process, coordinate design requirements through sub-subcommittees (such as music, Christian education, nursery, office, youth, interiors, fellowship, recreation, etc.), and to evaluate and recommend designs to the building committee and congregation.

*Architect/engineers—a team of professionals to develop several design options for presentation to the congregation, develop the church's ideas into plans and specifications that can be constructed, and observe the construction process to keep it in general conformance to the plans and specifications.

*Contractor and subcontractors—a team of professionals who construct the plans and specifications.

*Fund raiser—to guide the church through the steps of proper fund raising.

The key to the success of this structure is not just the overall theme but the details. Listen to every person who is interested in the design: the nursery workers, the youth group parents, the office staff—everyone. No one can be ignored, lest he or she become a squeaky wheel. As the planning process moves forward, the building committee and the architect must balance all the plates on the poles. Therefore, you desire an architect with big ears and flexible plans—one who will listen and respond. Expect to explore more than a few options, and expect to perfect one of the options through several revisions. Your final roundup depends on design compromises.

Once plans are agreed on, the roundup has occurred and moving them out and getting the building built is relatively easy—even if you are a novice. In the movie *City Slickers*, three urban "dudes" desired some adventure on a cowboy roundup and cattle drive. With the guidance of Curly, the seasoned professional, these three raw recruits learned the cowboy life and business. The same is true for church facilities design. A team composed of the congregation, a building committee, an architect, a contractor, and a fund raiser can work together to bring in a project.

South Suburban Christian Church (Disciples of Christ) in Littleton, Colorado, is an excellent example of organizing for operation. Their structure was shrinking from overuse. They felt the pain, so they went to a building doctor or architect.

The diagnosis was a pinched circulation pattern, weak education muscles, and a broken nose worship center. Their building was a relatively healthy structure, but these areas needed some rehabilitation. The circulation pattern required building precious parking and enlarging the loving lobby. The education spaces were reshuffled to pump up existing space to maximum utilization. And the broken nose worship required cosmetic surgery. It included repairing the platform and room acoustics.

The leaders rounded up and involved everyone interested in the design. As many as thirty people gave input, and a consensus plan was devised. They organized for operation by first recognizing the problem. Then, they sought professional help and had the surgery required. They continue to be a healthy, maturing ministry.

Making the House a Home

Shopping for a new house can be both joyous and burdensome. You consider location, schools, neighborhood, amenities, size of rooms, relationship between rooms, number of windows, and potential furniture layout. The list of objective requirements is endless. All must fit together to achieve the goal: making the house a home.

A home is a place where memories are built, relationships flourish, and life is lived to the fullest. This is much deeper than merely living in grand style. The same goes for church structures. For them to be home, they need life. "The spaces become places," as Herb Miller says.[22] Places where new people are welcomed and assimilated into tasks, small groups, and leadership positions. Places where people meet others, develop bonds, and encourage others to join and grow.

Therefore, organizing for operation goes beyond providing rooms. It anticipates and plans for greater involvement of more people. It organizes an accepting atmosphere and encourages visitors to become vital participants. Some churches stress spiritual gift education and utilization. Others have "recruitment officers" in adult classes to invite new members. Others assign church staff to follow through on "plugging in" people to ministry. The method is different for each church. The goal is the same: organized extroversion.

Countless movies have been made along this theme, such as *The War of the Roses,* in which a rich yuppie couple has every material possession but no love. Eventually, Mr. and Mrs. Rose angrily destroy their materials to spite each other. The same is true for churches. For them to grow, they require more than space and material goods. They require spaces that can become places—home places.

------------------- XII -------------------

EAGLE EYES

Only God can accurately predict what the twenty-first century will be like—and God is keeping most of it a secret. Our best guess is that tomorrow will be like today, only different. But we can catch a glimpse of the future, and we need to prepare for it.

History is like a rug being woven continuously. Many of the patterns of the 1990s will carry through to the year 2000—though they may not be exactly like the 1980s. Some patterns will change color, and some will change both color and form. But we will see little new history that did not evolve from today. Consequently, church leaders need to keep their heads up and their eyes directed forward, squinting to see as far into the future as possible. Like an eagle soaring on updrafts and scouring the territory for its next meal, they need to stay alert to the opportunities and challenges ahead.

In 1911, the first Indianapolis 500 produced amazing speeds of about 80 MPH. In 1960, the cars' improved mechanics raised the speed to about 140 MPH. In the 1990s the action flies by at over 200 MPH, nearly three times the blurs of 1911. At these speeds, the separation between a good race car driver and a great one is hundredths of a second.

There is little room for error. A lapse in concentration or a blink of an eye literally means hundreds of feet. So what makes a winner? Good equipment, of course, and an experienced driver. But the equipment and the driver must also be tuned to a good strategy, a strategy based on the predicted weather, track conditions, and the behaviors of other drivers.

Leading a church in today's world seems like racing in the Indianapolis 500. Everything is traveling faster. A great church needs the right equipment, crew, and driver(s), but it also needs a strategy based on the patterns of today and predictions for tomorrow. Here are some patterns and predictions that may be helpful to people who care about churches and for the buildings that house them.

Post-traditional Church. In 1937, 73 percent of all Americans were members of a church or synagogue. By 1988, membership had dropped to 65 percent. That membership slide touched mainline denominations more than others. But membership has increased or remained stable in some denominations, such as the Seventh Day Adventists, the Southern Baptists, the Assemblies of God, and independent churches.

According to *Church Growth Today* the twenty fastest growing churches in America in 1990 (based on worship attendance increases between 1989 and 1990) included eight independent, three Southern Baptist Convention, two Calvary Chapels, one National Baptist Convention (USA), one Church of God in Christ, one Christian and Missionary Alliance, one United Methodist, one Church of Christ, one Presbyterian Church in America, and one Reformed Church in America. On the list of the 99 fastest growing churches, we see only five mainline denominational churches: two United Methodists, two Presbyterian Church in America, and one American Baptist Church.[23] Elmer Towns calls this a shift to revolutionary methodology with conservative theology.

A second prominent aspect of the post-traditional church era is the increasing secularization of our society. The baby boomers are the first generation to deemphasize Judeo-Christian traditions and ethics. Thanksgiving has become

Turkey Day. The Christ Child of Christmas has been replaced by Santa Claus. Easter has the "resurrection" of a bunny rabbit. Secular humanists have halted school prayer and replaced it with a moment of silence. Many trend watchers think America is on the brink of becoming a twin sister of Western Europe. In France, 74 percent of the population are professing Roman Catholics, but only 6 percent practice the religion. The famous Gothic cathedrals have become houses of tourism and ceremony, not worship and fellowship.

Post-traditional church architecture is shifting away from high liturgy, symbolism, and sacredness toward utilitarian architecture. Earlier, we noted that the Cathedral of the Incarnation in Nashville, Tennessee, removed much of the ornate decorations that distract many baby boomers. Other examples include the hundreds of churches that are successfully meeting in schools, office buildings, and shopping centers. While some of the trend is related to financial restrictions (boomers tend to give about 20 percent less than their parents gave to churches), it also shows the new tolerance for a more non-religious atmosphere.

The utilitarian approach is most noticeable in worship spaces, but it is also seen in exterior facades and lobby spaces. In all of these areas, designers of newer buildings place greater importance on comfort and convenience than on a traditional architectural icon.

The growing governmental regulation book is another trend that affects the architectural arena. Undoubtedly influenced by the secularization of society, ever-increasing mounds of government red tape are hampering church architecture. For example, zoning and planning issues in one county restrict a local church's ability to install a free-standing bell tower. The leaders must also obtain permission on the type of material they can use, the height limitation, the set backs from the property lines, the landscaping plan, the location of a rainwater detention pond, and the size of the parking lot. Neighborhood opposition may restrict the membership size the church can reach. All of this is happening at an existing church site where owners are generally presumed to have a "right" to use their property as they see fit.

Other government interventions include handicap accessibility, day-care/preschool/private school regulations, and the life safety regulations of local building and fire departments. Some government oversight is good, especially to protect the public from organizations that jeopardize the health of their patrons. But many government officials are inclined to be distrustful and overstep their bounds. As we move into the twenty-first century, it is unlikely that these and accompanying influences of a post-traditional church era will diminish in their intensity.

Post-Yuppie. The life-style of most Americans has been changing for several years. Gone from our list of accepted norms are the self-indulgent power lunches and a win-at-business-at-all-costs mentality. These changes take many forms, among which the following are prominent.

Kids have replaced no kids. Baby boomers are bearing "boomlets" in record numbers. Family issues are coming to the forefront. Manufacturers now make many new products designed specifically for small children. Therefore, churches with quality children's programs and facilities will also benefit greatly.

Pursuit of passion has replaced pursuit of success. A deeply emotional worship service is as important as a deeply intellectual service. High touch and high participation—with clapping, holding hands, hugging, and high "fives"—have replaced stoic isolation in many church worship services.

Intelligent shoppers have replaced conspicuous consumers. Substance ministries are replacing the flash events. Meaningful programs and buildings have become more important than just show. Integrity and wisdom are virtuous characteristics that Christian leaders have always sought, and effective churches seem to give their pursuit more attention these days.

Home bodies have replaced workaholics. A saying of the 1980s went "We worship our work, work at our play, and play at our worship." The 1990s motto that replaced it is "Pizzahut, pizza to go." Family and friends have leapfrogged work and money as personal priorities. Churches that reinforce relationships will continue to minister successfully, because they connect with those felt needs. Some churches have family Bible study groups. Many are developing home studies. Others are building recreation centers for sports and entertainment. Cry rooms have become popular again. Picnic and family retreat centers will also become important in the future.

The end of the yuppie years has not ended the desire to have fun. Americans' appetite for thrill and enjoyment keeps on growing. Vacation home sales continue to rise, creating a city and church vacancy on Sunday. We also are spending more money on entertainment than on clothes these days, creating a huge Christian entertainment industry. And recreational sports are still in high demand. The over-thirty weekend sports warrior continues to thrive. All of these areas can affect building design.

America is graying. More people are living longer, and a larger percentage of Americans are over sixty years of age. But something else even bigger than that is happening to demographic composites. The young and carefree days of the boomers' twenties and thirties will soon be replaced by the "responsible fifties" for those born in 1946. That aging process is bound to create some mid-life crisis and pre-retirement planning. It will also create a huge power base. Boomers make up a large portion of middle management in corporate America. A boomer named Bill Clinton in 1993 took control of the White House; soon boomers will control the upper management of companies like AT&T, IBM, and CBS. They are increasing their influence on church life as well. A large percentage of them attend church on a regular basis. In many congregations, they are beginning to develop a huge power base and are influencing church structures. That influence will grow.

Several churches have responded by targeting boomers. Elmer Towers describes these institutions as "baby boomer churches." He believes 3,000 to 4,000 churches are pastored by boomers to reach boomers. Their characteristics generally include:

High touch and high feel worship
Contemporary music
Pastoral leadership to make every member a minister
Businesslike, efficient operations and methods
Two hours of adult attendance, with home oriented studies
No Sunday evening services
Low financial giving
Practical, teaching sermons[24]

Even if your church is not a "boomer church," it cannot ignore their influence. Boomers want the best. They will not attend a second-rate ministry in second-rate buildings. They are turned off by out-of-key musicians and unpolished, insincere speakers.

Demand for Choices. In 1990 there were 375,000 churches in America. About one-half of these organizations had less than seventy-five attenders. In contrast, the largest 14 percent of the churches have 50 percent of the churchgoers. The reason for these contrasts is that people desire choices and full-service churches.

Most churches that begin to offer a second worship service in another style and time slot increase their overall attendance. People also want a variety of ministry options, designed to help others and to help meet their own particular needs. Therefore, multiple Bible studies, fellowship groups, support groups, and Sunday school classes are a successful method. Because of these and other changes, staff sizes are growing. In 1960 the common ratio was one pastor per every 300 active members. That number had changed to one pastor per 150 members by 1990. Some say it will reach one pastor per 100 members by the year 2000.

These trends profoundly affect architecture. Church buildings have changed from cute country cottages to sprawling complex campuses. A successful 250-person church had better plan for building expansion, because good multiple ministry churches attract people like honey attracts flies. Five acres of land is the absolute minimal land parcel—ten is much better. And instead of building additions haphazardly, each phase needs careful planning because it will affect future additions. Church complexes are more than a sanctuary with a tiny office and nursery. They need planning for classrooms, multiple offices, dining facilities, recreation areas, and even retreat centers.

In this kind of setting, the architectural style should focus on lasting several generations. The style should age well and be capable of adjusting to changing events. Timelessness has always been an important feature in architecture, but it is even more so in today's church.

Minorities Becoming Majorities. The minority population continues to grow in America. By the year 2000 non-whites will be a majority in California. Demographers are predicting that minorities will surpass whites in the total population of the United States by the year 2015. White middle-income America is becoming extinct. Therefore, many of the old strategies designed to reach these persons are becoming obsolete as well.

John Vaughan's research indicates that eight of the twelve fastest growing churches in America in 1989 were black congregations.[25] This vast potential market continues to multiply. Denominations that diversify their strategies will numerically explode into the twenty-first century.

Flexibility for the Twenty-first Century

In auto racing, a yellow flag means caution, accident ahead. A great strategy has one more essential element that functions when life's yellow flags occur. These incidents are always traumatic and unexpected, yet are virtually inevitable. But to a great race car driver, yellow flags also mean there is great opportunity—a chance to get refueled when cars are traveling slower—a chance to move up behind the leader. Great drivers also know that yellow flags can be tragic to drivers who are not directly involved in the accident, if a driver ignores the opportunity.

Churches are in similar situations. They are tooling along in the ministry race, when all of a sudden a crisis occurs—a local factory shuts down, or a tornado wipes out huge chunks of town. In an instant, a yellow flag arises, and your past strategy is worthless. You have two choices: You can pretend nothing happened and lose an opportunity, or you can flex and become stronger.

Church buildings need to be flexible. The only perfect building is one that can accommodate change—change that can add staff offices to accommodate a growing demand for family counseling; change to a different music style that requires adding microphones for a soloist or quartet; change brought on by an unusually large first- and second-grade class that requires more space. Adaptability is the key to success: moving walls, changing decorations, maintaining multi-use centers, expanding seating. Church buildings are a lot like a shopping center, where an electronic store grows and rents an additional stall or a clothing store goes out of business. The building is in a constant state of flux. The structural, mechanical, and electrical systems are also required to respond to flux. They must be designed so that the ceiling lights can be changed for a new room use. The mechanical ducts must sometimes be shifted to add a wall and adjust the air volume. Structural walls should not hamper remodeling, and the wall finishes must be adaptable enough to allow "tenants" to redecorate.

John Maxwell, pastor at Skyline Wesleyan Church in San Diego, states: "Growth equals change, because you cannot grow unless you change. Change is the price we pay for growth."[26] Maxwell knows that is the role of a church growth pastor: be a change agent.

Leith Anderson, Pastor at Wooddale Church in Minneapolis and author of *Dying for Change,* reminds us: "Jesus was and is the greatest change agent in the universe, He changes sinners into saints. He then forms those saints into the church. Christ's church is extraordinary—changing with every generation yet keeping the Gospel truth unchanged."[27]

By God's grace we will build church structures that build up Christ's extraordinary church.

APPENDIX

TWENTY IMPROVEMENTS FOR UNDER
THREE HUNDRED DOLLARS CHECKLIST

____ 1. Add colorful landscaping.
____ 2. Add exterior Christmas lights.
____ 3. Assign visitor and elderly parking.
____ 4. Provide stacked parking stalls.
____ 5. Provide hospitality center.
____ 6. Provide seating area in lobby.
____ 7. During comfortable weather, build fellowship tent.
____ 8. Install cheerful flowers, bulletin board, and/or banners in lobby.
____ 9. Redecorate nursery.
____ 10. Restock nursery toys.
____ 11. Provide qualified nursery staff.
____ 12. Hang announcement board at nursery counter.
____ 13. Decorate worship center with sermon topic.
____ 14. Provide periodic festive atmosphere in worship.
____ 15. Decorate classrooms with current children's work.
____ 16. Provide bulletin boards in adult rooms for future or recent events and announcements.
____ 17. Repaint classrooms.
____ 18. Provide handicap parking.
____ 19. Provide ramp entrance(s) to building.
____ 20. Install wheelchair locations in sanctuary.

EXALTING EXTERIOR CHECKLIST

___ ___ ___   1. Maintenance items needing repair?
___ ___ ___   2. Landscape at least 20 percent of property.
                  3. Soften entrances with
                    a. Awnings or banners.
___ ___ ___   b. Fountain.
___ ___ ___   c. Patio lighting, furniture, and
                    landscaping.
                  4. Significant signs.
___ ___ ___   a. Perpendicular to road.
___ ___ ___   b. Large simple lettering.
___ ___ ___   c. Display without interference.
___ ___ ___   d. Drop denominational name.
___ ___ ___   e. Display church logo.
___ ___ ___   5. Construct attractive exterior architecture.

PRECIOUS PARKING CHECKLIST

_____ 1. Buy land and expand parking.
_____ 2. Build parking garage.
_____ 3. Rent parking from nearby structure.
4. Pave parking lot:
_____ a. With proper slopes.
_____ b. Install curbs or wheel stops.
_____ c. Paint striping.
_____ d. Rainwater detention.
_____ 5. Add directional signs.
_____ 6. Keep snow-plowed.
_____ 7. Provide lighting.

A ROYAL LOBBY CHECKLIST

——— 1. Expand lobby to 1/3 area of sanctuary.
2. Add intimate appeal:
———   a. Plants.
———   b. Water feature.
———   c. Seating.
———   d. Fireplace.
———   e. Carpeting.
——— 3. Provide central access to building.
——— 4. Add directional signs.
——— 5. Recondition restrooms.
——— 6. Add natural light via skylights or windows.
——— 7. Raise ceiling.
——— 8. Hang banners and bulletin boards.
——— 9. Construct information and sign-up counter.
——— 10. Locate library in lobby or provide library cart.

A NURTURING NURSERY CHECKLIST

__ __ __   1. Locate nursery and preschool rooms off lobby.

__ __ __   2. Provide drop-off/storage counter.

__ __ __   3. Construct diaper changing counter.

__ __ __   4. Allocate thirty to thirty-five square feet per child.

                 5. Environmental amenities:

__ __ __   a. Proper heating and cooling.

__ __ __   b. Carpeting.

__ __ __   c. Natural light.

__ __ __   d. Cheerful colors.

__ __ __   e. Soundproofing walls, floor, and ceiling.

__ __ __   f. Outdoor play area.

__ __ __   6. Numbering system.

__ __ __   7. Cry room.

APPENDIX

A CELEBRATION CENTER CHECKLIST

1. Provide projector and screen system.
2. Platform flexibility for different sizes of groups and types of services.
3. Appropriate room acoustics for song, music, and speech.
4. Lighten finish colors in paint, stain, floor, and pew coverings.
5. Remove cluttered religious icons.
6. Provide comfortable platform atmosphere.
7. Use wireless microphone for pastor.
8. Install properly designed sound system.
9. Rearrange seating for intimacy to platform and wrap-around seating.
10. Remove furniture barriers at platform.
11. Add natural light through windows or skylights.
12. Increase light levels with direct and indirect light.
13. Expand or reduce amount of seating to comfortable level.
14. Increase distance to three feet for each row of seats.
15. Provide a minimum of 5 percent of room surfaces in changing decorations.

INCORPORATION ROOMS CHECKLIST

  __ __ __   1. Provide comfortable small support group rooms.

  __ __ __   2. Construct banquet dining facilities.

  __ __ __   3. Install athletic facilities for basketball, softball, volleyball, etc.

  __ __ __   4. Provide space for community services—i.e., clothing or food bank, homeless shelter, elderly housing, school facilities, child care, or community groups.

               5. Provide proper amount, type, and location of education space:

  __ __ __   a. Visual buffer.

  __ __ __   b. Acoustical buffer.

  __ __ __   c. Cheerful carpeting and wall colors.

  __ __ __   d. Proper lighting.

  __ __ __   e. Tables, chairs, and equipment as needed.

  __ __ __   f. Well ventilated, heated, and cooled.

ALTERATION ALTERNATIVES CHECKLIST

__ __ __   1. Add additional services or educational hours.

__ __ __   2. Rearrange room use for maximum efficiency.

__ __ __   3. Use appropriate furniture and arrangement for maximum use.

__ __ __   4. Convert "out of the way" locations into usable rooms.

5. Create multiple use facilities:

__ __ __   a. Classrooms.

__ __ __   b. Sanctuary/fellowship hall/recreation area.

6. Relocate some rooms off campus:

__ __ __   a. Storage.

__ __ __   b. Small groups/classrooms.

__ __ __   c. Offices.

7. Add on if:

__ __ __   a. Visibility is high.

__ __ __   b. Access is major.

__ __ __   c. Acreage is available.

__ __ __   d. Site is buildable.

__ __ __   e. Location is for ministry.

__ __ __   f. Architecture is healthy.

__ __ __   g. Increases salability.

__ __ __   h. Financial burden is bearable.

__ __ __   i. Open mind-set.

NOTES

1. Robert C. Bast *The Missing Generation* (New York and Monrovia, Calif.: Reformed Church of America and Church Growth, Inc., 1991), p. 116.

2. Hans Finzel, *Help! I'm a Baby Boomer* (Wheaton, Ill.: Victor Books, 1989), p. 144.

3. Cathy Cummins, "Burger Magnate Girdles Globe," *Denver Post*, November 5, 1991, p. 3C.

4. Elmer Towns, *Ten of Today's Most Innovative Churches* (Ventura, Calif.: Regal Books, 1990), p. 62.

5. David McCandless, "Acoustic Wall Hangings," *Faith and Form* (Fall 1991): 27-28.

6. *Environment and Art in Catholic Worship*, National Conference of Catholic Bishops, Bishop's Committee on the Liturgy (Chicago: Liturgy Training Publications, 1986), p. 4.

7. Gwenn E. McCormick, *Designing Worship Centers* (Nashville: Convention Press, 1988), p. 7.

8. Arthur Pierce Middleton, *New Wine in Old Skins* (Wilton, Conn.: Morehouse-Barlow, 1988), p. 23.

9. Towns, *Ten of Today's Most Innovative Churches.*

10. "Renovated Church Reflects Changing Image," *Commercial Renovation* (October 1988): 32.

11. Herb Miller, *The Vital Congregation* (Nashville: Abingdon Press, 1990), p. 30.

12. Daniel Coleman, "Emotions Contagious, Study Says," *The Denver Post*, October 20, 1991, p. 26A.

13. Flavil R. Yeakley, Jr. "Adult Bible Classes and Church Growth," *Church Growth Today* 6, 2 (1991): 2.

119

254.7
L479 LINCOLN CHRISTIAN COLLEGE AND SEMINARY 89004

NOTES

14. Win Arn, *The Church Growth Ratio Book* (Pasadena, Calif.: Church Growth, Inc., 1987), pp. 23-25, 31.

15. Miller, *The Vital Congregation*, p. 96.

16. William Morris, *The American Heritage Dictionary* (New York: American Heritage Publishing Co., 1969), p. 784.

17. Joseph Miller, "Blueprints for Growth," *The Church Planter* 2, 1 (1987): 4.

18. Office of Attorney General, *Federal Register* 56, 144, Section 36.402 (July 26, 1991): 35600.

19. Ibid., Section 36.405, p. 35601.

20. Miller, *The Vital Congregation*, p. 38.

21. Ray Bowman and Eddy Hall, "How to Maximize Your Current Space," *Your Church*, July and August 1991, pp. 9-11.

22. Herb Miller, "Maintaining Your Place-Space Balance," *Net Results* 13, 2 (February 1992): 3.

23. John N. Vaughan, "North America's Fastest Growing Churches 1989–1990," *Church Growth Today*, 6, 6 (1991): 2-3.

24. Elmer Towns, "Reading the Baby Boomer," *Church Growth Today* 5, 5 (1990): 1-3.

25. Vaughan, "North America's Fastest Growing Churches 1989–1990," p. 1.

26. Towns, "Reading the Baby Boomer," p. 27.

27. Leith Anderson, *Dying for Change* (Minneapolis: Bethany House, 1990), p. 207.